A History of
EWELL

The Epsom and Ewell coat of arms: the horses' heads represent the Epsom races, the wavy lines at the bottom are blue and represent the Ewell springs on the white chalk. Reproduced by kind permission of the Epsom and Ewell Borough Council.

A History of EWELL

Charles Abdy

Phillimore

1992

Published by
PHILLIMORE & CO. LTD.
Shopwyke Hall, Chichester, Sussex

ISBN 0 85033 840 9

Printed and bound in Great Britain by
BIDDLES LTD.
Guildford, Surrey

Contents

List of Illustrations

Frontispiece: The Epsom and Ewell coat of arms

Illustration Acknowledgements

Bourne Hall Museum, 3-7, 12-16, 18, 21, 28, 30, 31, 47-50, 56, 59, 61-68, 70, 71, 73, 79, 80, 82, 84, 90, 91, 97, 98, 100, 102-104, 108, 109, 111-113, 115, 118, 120, 124, 125, 127-129, 132, 134; Ewell United Reformed Church, 33, 74, 75, 78; Glyn House Administration, 55, 57; Bourne Hall Library, 17, 34-36, 38, 45, 46, 51, 69, 81, 92, 99, 106, 119, 130, 136, 137, 139.

Unless otherwise indicated, the photographs were taken by the author, including photographs of museum artifacts.

Acknowledgements

I would like to express my warm thanks to the following: The Curator of Bourne Hall Museum, Jeremy Harte, for being always willing to point me in the right direction and make available material for photographs. The staff of Bourne Hall Library for dealing with my many requests for recondite information with patience and efficiency and making old photographs available. Mr. Geoffrey Berry, Clerk and Treasurer of the Ewell Parochial Trusts (Relief in Need), for the information on which Chapter 13 is based. Mr. Maurice Exwood, for advice concerning mathematical tiles. Mr. Denis McCann, for photographs relating to railways. Mr. Clive Orton, for information on the King William IV excavations. Mr. E. A. Sparrow, for information on the Jameson engineering company. Mr. Trevor White, for information on Captain C. Wiener at Ewell Castle. The members of local churches who provided information. The Surrey Archaeological Society for permission to include extracts from the article 'Ewell in 1577' published in S.A.C. Volume 54. The Surrey Record Society for permission to include extracts from their publication on Fitznell's Cartulary.

Members of the Nonsuch Antiquarian Society, more fully referred to in the Introduction. Last but by no means least, Barbara, for her invaluable contributions, both in digging out information and typing my not always very legible drafts.

Introduction

When my wife Barbara and I moved to Ewell in 1982 we found many things to remind us that it had not always been a modern dormitory suburb. There were old jettied houses in the High Street which must surely be Tudor and stately Georgian buildings in Spring Street and Church Street. The imposing gateway of Bourne Hall was a statement about a way of life quite different to that of today. A visit to Bourne Hall Museum introduced us to the Roman dimension — the many artefacts from that period, fine pottery, brooches, coins, even gaming counters, painted a picture of a stable community that had been thriving more than fifteen hundred years ago. This evidence of an eventful past kindled a desire to know something of the history of Ewell which led to our joining the Nonsuch Antiquarian Society. We asked what histories had been published and were told about the book that had been written by Cloudesley Willis in 1931. It was, and still is, a mine of information, with particular emphasis on what the village was like around the turn of the century. There was also a mass of material that had been gathered together by members of the Nonsuch Antiquarian Society, which was conceived during the major excavation of Nonsuch Palace and born in 1960, information that had not been available to Cloudesley Willis.

Largely for our own benefit, to make some sort of sense out of the heterogeneous collection of facts, and to relate it to present-day Ewell, we put together a slide show that we presented to the Society in May 1991. Several members asked whether it could be published in book form. Mabel Dexter of the Society's Documentary Group commented 'It has been said that although the past does not change, its history has to be written afresh in each generation. More than a generation has passed since Cloudesley Willis published his pioneering *History of Ewell*. Dare we hope that we have among our members someone who will become Ewell's historian for the 1990s?' That was a challenge that could not be ignored, and this book is the result. The original talk has been added to, but as the structure seemed to work well it has been retained. The fact that we had already established a framework for our history was a tremendous help. In truth, history is rather a grand word to apply to what is little more than a compilation of an album of snapshots of the past, verbal and photographic. The guiding principle in selecting the snapshots has been to give a sense of the general course of events over the centuries.

Access to the records of the Nonsuch Antiquarian Society, many of which have been published as Occasional Papers, was of prime importance, and I acknowledge with gratitude the help given by the Secretary, Peggy Bedwell, and other members of the Society, in particular those belonging to the Documentary Group. Special mention must be made of Mabel Dexter, whose knowledge of Ewell is truly encyclopaedic, and the late Phyllis Davies whose contributions to the Occasional Papers were numerous.

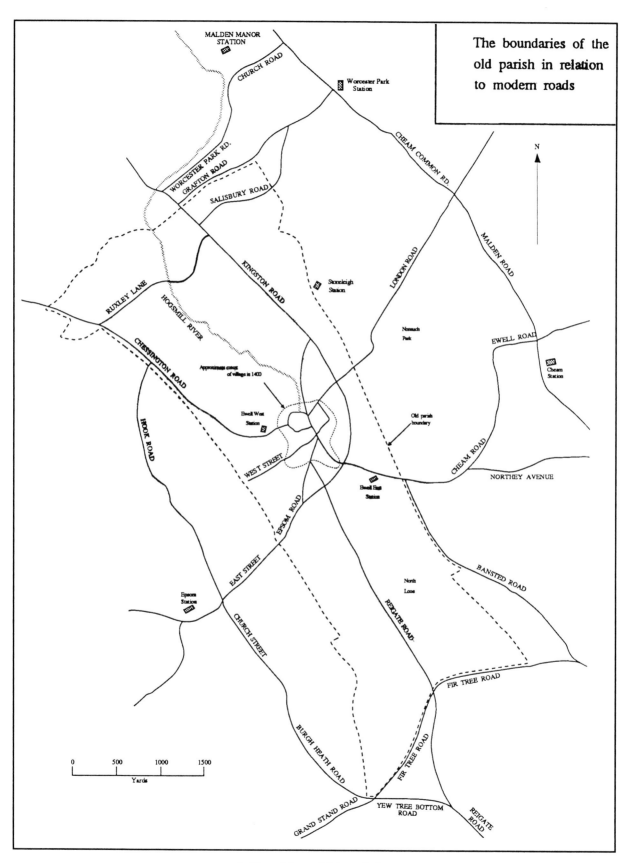

1. Map of the parish boundaries

Chapter 1

The Development of the Parish

The springs of pure water at Ewell that were the source of the River Hogsmill attracted man from the earliest times.[1] The village is at the foot of the gentle slope of the north side of the North Downs, where the chalk dips beneath the London clay. Between the chalk and the clay are layers of sand and gravel, and that is where the water that had collected in the chalk met the impermeable clay and gushed up from the ground. The name Ewell is derived from the Saxon for river-spring.

Local historian, Cloudesley Willis, writing around 1930, said that the flow of the Hogsmill, measured at the Upper Mill, was four and a half million gallons a day and that it took six months for the water to come down the hills to the springs. The abundant water and the ready supply of flints from the chalk made Ewell a highly desirable locality for Stone Age man and numerous Mesolithic flint workings, possibly going back to 8,000 B.C. have been found. Although Mesolithic man was a nomadic hunter, not given to lengthy settlement in one place, the abundance of remains suggests that he made frequent use of the area. There is also evidence of Neolithic and Bronze Age occupation, while the Iron Age is well represented by finds of pottery and implements in what were clearly Celtic settlements. The Romans also appreciated the amenities of the country and there was an extensive Romano-British settlement.

The Saxons divided Surrey into parishes, attempting to make each a viable agricultural unit by taking into account the terrain, which led to parishes to the north and south of the North Downs being laid out as north to south strips. Ewell, in the Hundred of Copthorne, is typical of the parishes to the north and it takes in London clay, sand and gravel and then chalk downland. Epsom, Cuddington, Cheam, Sutton and Carshalton are some of the other parishes that were arranged in this manner. Some of the parishes and manors had 'outliers' in the Weald to give the villagers access to swine grazing. Ewell had several such outliers and it also had Kingswood, a wooded area on the Downs some two miles south of the parish boundary which was part of the parish of Ewell until the last century. The parish, excluding outliers, was nearly four miles from north to south and almost a mile wide. The village was very near the centre of the Parish. The main arable land was to the south, while north of the village was largely meadows and common land. The extreme south and south-east were the common downs.

This history is concerned with Ewell within the old parish boundaries.

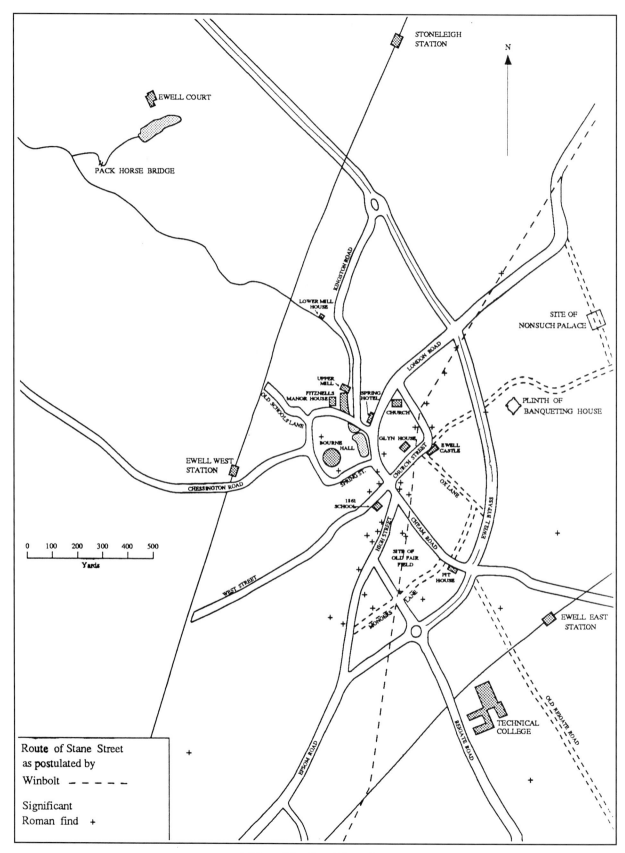

2. Map of Ewell and Stane Street

Chapter 2

Roman Ewell

When the Romans invaded this country in A.D. 43 they set about building roads to assist with troop movements and trade. The road from London Bridge to Chichester that we now call Stane Street is believed to have been made during the first decade or so after the invasion, but it was not until the 1930s that evidence was found to prove that it passed through Ewell; the *Victoria History of Surrey* of 1902 said, 'Ewell lay possibly on the Roman road'.

The rediscovery of Stane Street owes much to three men, S. E. Winbolt, I. D. Margary and A.W. G. Lowther. Winbolt made a thorough exploration of Stane Street and published his findings in *With a spade on Stane Street,* in 1936. Margary was the great authority on Roman roads in the South East and covered Stane Street thoroughly in *Roman Ways in the Weald*, published in 1948, acknowledging his debt to Winbolt. Lowther was a local man who made notable contributions to Iron Age and Roman studies in Surrey, including an important monograph on the classification of Roman flue tiles. He worked with Winbolt on the excavations in the Old Fair Field in Ewell in 1933 which revealed a considerable portion of Stane Street. Anthony Lowther died in 1972 and is buried in the churchyard of St Mary's, Ewell.

Although Stane Street passes through Ewell Village it is not on the line of present-day streets; in fact, even the medieval roads disregarded the Roman road. The course in relation to modern roads, based on the findings of Winbolt and Margary, can be seen on the map. More recent work suggests that adjustments should be made here and there, but the road shown is believed to be substantially correct. London Road approaching Ewell is on the line of Stane Street: traces of the agger are to be seen in the plantation on the north west of Nonsuch Park, but at Briarwood Road the modern roads leave the old road and do not pick it up again until south of Dorking, if we exclude the rough track of Pebble Lane south of Epsom.

It is generally assumed that the Romans arranged the route of Stane Street so as to take advantage of the springs at Ewell for fresh water, but in fact, if the springs had not been there, their chosen route would still have been a good one, bearing in mind the way it made use of the gap in the North Downs provided by the Mole Valley. Furthermore, as pointed out by S. E.Winbolt, the deviation in the route in the vicinity of Ewell took advantage of the geology: the change of direction brings the road onto the chalk quicker and avoids some of the more difficult Woolwich Beds and Thanet Sands.

There is no doubt that there was a sizeable Romano-British settlement at Ewell as a great deal of Roman pottery and other artefacts including hundreds of coins have been excavated over various sites, the most important of which are shown on the map. It may also have been a posting station, with shelter and provisions for officials and other users of Stane Street. Remains of such stations have been found at Hardham and Alfoldean at distances of 13 and 25 miles from Chichester, and it is thought that there would have been a station at Dorking and another between Dorking and London, probably at Merton, but possibly at Ewell.

VESPASIAN 69-79			SEVERUS ALEXANDER 222-235		
TRAJAN 98-117			GALLIENUS 253-268		
HADRIAN 117-138			POSTHUMUS 260-268		
ANTONINUS PIUS 138-161			CLAUDIUS GOTHICUS 268-269		
MARCUS AURELIUS 161-180			VICTORINUS 269-271		
COMMODUS 176-192			TETRICUS I AND II 271-273		
SEPTIMIUS SEVERUS 193-211			CONSTANTINE I 307-337		

3 & 4. Roman coins, found during the excavations on the *King William IV* site in 1967-77, covered a large part of the Roman occupation of Britain.

5 & 6. Bone gaming counters and a burial urn found near North Looe in an excavation that started in 1946. Some of the counters had faint scratched inscriptions on the back, one interpretation of which was 'of Remus', and so the occupant of the urn is popularly known as Remus. The burial urn contained ashes that were most probably those of a boy buried in the second century.

Perhaps the best evidence of the occupation of Ewell in Roman times is the many coins: those illustrated came from just one site, the *King William IV*, and cover the period of the Roman occupation of Britain with only a few gaps. Roman remains have been found at more than 50 sites in Ewell since the first recorded excavation in 1847, and there have been numerous chance surface finds. Traces of at least eight buildings have been unearthed, and many rubbish pits. Ditches that may have been associated with the boundaries have also been discovered. Recent finds of Roman artefacts around one of the springs that were the source of the Hogsmill River could be connected with votive offerings.

Settlement in the Roman period was not restricted to the centre of what became Ewell village in the immediate vicinity of Stane Street. Romano-British remains have been dug up at places remote from the road, one such site being near North Looe, about a mile to the south of the village and three quarters of a mile to the east of the road. The excavations that started in 1946 gave evidence of a small farmstead, the features of which included three Iron Age 'beehive' storage pits, drainage gullies and pottery, the earliest being pre-Roman, possibly as early as the fifth century B.C. There was also later pre-Roman pottery, and Roman material covering a good part of the occupation. There were even fragments of medieval and post-medieval pottery suggesting that there was more or less continuous occupation of the site for something like two thousand years. Associated with the farmstead was the burial of a young man named Remus; at least that is how he is known by some local archaeologists. His ashes were found in a wide-mouthed jar of brown earthenware. A British Museum expert identified the fragment of calcined bone as probably belonging to a young male and suggested a burial date of the second century. In and around the jar were nine bone gaming counters, six of which carried a scratched inscription, one suggested interpretation of which was 'of Remus'. The skeleton of a dog was found nearby, so there is a possibility that the young boy was buried with his favourite game and his pet dog.

The full significance of Roman Ewell has still to be assessed. Victorian theories that it might be the 'lost city of Canca of the Geographer of Ravenna' or the 'Noviomagus of Ptolemy' have been discounted, but its importance as a settlement on Stane Street is beyond dispute.

Chapter 3

Excavations in Ewell

The archaeological excavations in Ewell are of particular importance for the information they provide on Roman and earlier periods. Unfortunately, some of the diggers have been more enthusiastic with the spade than with the pen and not all of their work has been properly recorded. However, a considerable amount of information is being built up and, to illustrate what has been achieved, brief accounts are given of excavations at two sites, Purberry Shot and the *King William IV*.

Purberry Shot

Excavations were carried out in 1938-9 by A. W. G.Lowther on the site of a house known as Purberry Shot, where a block of flats was to be built. Purberry Shot is towards the southern end of Ewell village, on the west side of the Epsom road, approximately 200 yards from Stane Street. It was a very productive dig and yielded finds from the Mesolithic, Bronze and Iron Ages as well as Roman and medieval periods. There was evidence of extensive flint and iron working activity. There was a great deal of Iron-Age pottery and Roman pottery, much of which was found in a well that went down to a depth of more than 40 ft. through Thanet sand and chalk.

7. The large Iron-Age pot from Purberry Shot.

Finds from the late Iron Age included remains of timber huts and an exceptionally large pot. The Roman pottery covered a wide range of dates and types, including imported Samian ware. Surprisingly, only three coins were found. The medieval finds were excavated from the top-soil and were fragments of pottery that dated back to the 11th and 12th centuries.

A road appears to have been built across the site in about A.D. 150. It was about 22 ft. wide and ran in a north-easterly direction, so that it would have intersected the route of Stane Street. It was under more than two feet of topsoil, which, together with the absence of Saxon artefacts, may account for the road going out of use. Possibly there was a period after the Romans left when parts of Ewell were deserted. Much of the village is low-lying and could well have been subject to flooding from the springs that were the source of the Hogsmill. This would be conducive to a build-up of silt that would soon obliterate the roads.

8. This well head was erected over a Roman well following excavations by A. W. G. Lowther on the site of the house known as Purberry Shot in 1938-9.

9. The *King William IV* in the High Street was built in the early 19th century on the site of an earlier public house. The name changed from the *George and Dragon* soon after William IV came to the throne. Extensive Roman remains were found in the garden in 1967-77.

King William IV

One of the most productive digs in Ewell was at the back of the *King William IV* public house and adjacent buildings in the High Street and Cheam Road. It went on between 1967 and 1977 under various directors and unearthed a vast collection of animal bones, pottery, building materials and miscellaneous artefacts. In all there were some 250 boxes of finds, including about 100 boxes of pottery of which roughly 75 per cent was Roman. The site was just to the west of the assumed route of Stane Street.

The prehistoric material recovered included flints, a neolithic/early bronze age beaker and fragments of Iron-Age pots. Much of the Roman material came from two 'back-filled' wells, and numerous pits. There were over 33,000 sherds of pottery dating from the first to the late fourth century, with the late second and the third century predominating and from a variety of sources. There was East Gaulish samian, a glazed ware cup from Lyon and a Palestinian amphora.

The considerable quantity of building material included greensand blocks, tile and brick, daub and wall plaster which came mostly from the back-filled wells and pits, and suggests that there had been a substantial building nearby. The bones of domestic animals were also discovered, cattle being the most common, but there were also pigs, sheep and the bones of a number of edible birds.

One of the most exciting finds was a hoard of coins of about A.D. 270, found in a bronze flagon at the bottom of a well, which also produced an assortment of ironwork including manacles.

Post-Roman pottery included one sherd of Saxon and some medieval, Tudor and 18th-century pottery.

10. Work in progress in 1968 on the *King William IV* archaeological excavation in Ewell. It went on for ten years and unearthed a vast collection of pottery, building materials and miscellaneous artefacts, much of it Roman.

11. Work on the *King William IV* site in 1970. The pits and wells investigated required deep excavations.

12. Roman pottery from the *King William IV* excavation, from left to right, a bowl in red/black earthenware, a jar and a folded beaker, both in greyware.

13. Roman pottery from the *King William IV* excavation, a bowl of pink earthenware, and a greyware pitcher with pink slip.

14. Two small objects from the *King William IV* excavation that went on from 1967 to 1977, on the left a brooch, grey and green enamel on bronze, and on the right a seal box lid, bronze inlaid with grey and green stone, probably second century A.D.

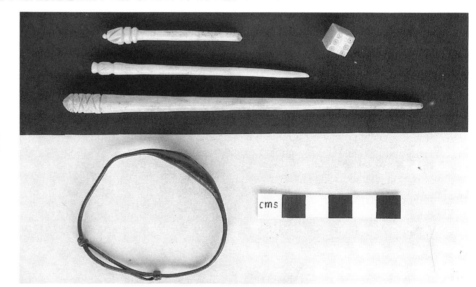

15. From the *King William IV* excavation, bone pins, a die and a bronze bracelet.

16. From the *King William IV* excavation, a bone needle, a tin plated bronze spoon for eating shell fish, and a nail cleaner.

Chapter 4

Saxon Ewell

We know that after the Romans left the Saxons moved in, but documentary evidence is scarce. The Venerable Bede omitted to make any reference to Ewell, and we have to deduce what things were like from more general information and archaeology.

It would seem that the Britons made some attempt to defend themselves against Saxon invaders after the Roman army withdrew. In fact the monk Gildas referred to a British victory against the Saxons at Mons Badonicus in A.D. 500, although it has not been possible to determine where this was. However, early in the sixth century Saxon settlements were well established, the earliest in Surrey, being in the north, because the raiders came along the Thames. The Saxon burial grounds at Croydon, Beddington and Mitcham are among the most ancient in the Thames Basin. They also came down the River Wey and the Wey Valley became a primary region of settlement. Godalming and Woking are Saxon names. If the Hogsmill River was not wide enough to be of use to the Saxons, they could well have made use of Stane Street, since it was used by William the Conqueror in 1066 and it seems likely that there would have been an early settlement in the neighbourhood of Ewell.

The main archaeological evidence of Saxon settlement is an extensive cemetery in the Grove and Ewell House area. The first known reference is in John Aubrey's *Natural History and Antiquities of the County of Surrey*, published in 1718 which said that human bones had been unearthed in the grounds of Ewell House. In 1930 three burials were found when a trench for an electric cable was taken along The Grove. There were more finds in 1932, and in 1934 when Lowther and Winbolt carried out excavations. In all, at least 12 burials were found with grave goods that included knives, spearheads, shield bosses, rings and brooches. Some of these burials were cinerary urns, but bodies were also found, including one having a west-east orientation, which suggests that the cemetery was in use through pagan and Christian periods.

17. The grove of lime trees between the High Street and West Street in 1924. It was said to have been planted in honour of King William III when he came to the throne in 1689. There are still some lime trees along the Grove.

11

18. A Saxon bronze hanging bowl from a barrow at Gally Hills, Banstead Down, excavated in 1972. The string around the rim has been preserved by impregnation with corrosion products from the bronze.

Further graves have been discovered cut in the chalk of the Downs to the south of the Ewell parish boundary. One of these excavated in 1972 was in the group of four barrows known as the Gally Hills on Banstead Down and contained the lower half of the skeleton of a tall young warrior buried with a knife, spear, shield and a bronze bowl. The top half of the skeleton is thought to have been destroyed when a hole was dug for a gallows post in medieval times. Five skeletons showing signs of hanging were found nearby. As recently as 1986 more than 40 Saxon graves dating back to probably the late sixth or early seventh century have been uncovered following a discovery during development work at Tadworth.

There is considerable uncertainty as to the origin of the Saxons who settled in the Ewell area: whereas some of the grave goods are comparable with material found in the Wandle cemeteries at Croydon, Beddington and Mitcham, some experts have suggested that the area was settled by the South Saxons pushing north. Furthermore, in medieval times the local unit of land measurement was the juger, equivalent to 13 acres, which was the unit of the Jutes of Kent, and not the virgate which was the usual Saxon unit, suggesting possible settlement from the east.

The Saxons of Surrey have no independent history and at different periods of the seventh century Surrey was a province of Kent, Wessex and Mercia in turn. There is a strong possibility that Surrey had earlier been part of a Middle Saxon kingdom which included Middlesex and Essex. The name Surrey means southern district and it is assumed that it refers to the southern district of the Middle Saxons.

The efforts of Augustine to convert the English to Christianity were remarkably successful, and by 660 it was the dominant religion. It was King Ethelred who supported Augustine when he arrived in Canterbury in 596, and from then on there was a close association between the church, kings and the state. Theodore of Tarsus came to Canterbury in 669 and is traditionally credited with organising dioceses and parishes. Chertsey Abbey was founded in 675, and the first mention of Ewell is in the foundation charter when 30 mansas of land in Ewell and Cuddington were granted to the new abbey by Frithwald, the under-king of Surrey. It has to be said that the charter exists only in a mid-13th-century copy, and there is some doubt as to the validity of the claim.

The basis of Saxon society was the peasant landholder, subject to no lord but the king. But kings granted lands and services to their retainers, the thegns, who became lords of innumerable villages. The peasant landholders lost their economic and personal independence and by 1066 the greater part of Southern England was divided into manors largely inhabited by serfs and slaves. The foundations had been laid for the manorial economy of the Middle Ages and when the Normans invaded, the main fabric of English life was already in place. Most of the country's county boundaries had been fixed and remained as such until the changes of recent times. With the arrival of the Normans, Saxon lords were replaced by their Norman or French counterparts, although in a few cases some Saxons were allowed to keep their lands.

At the time of the conquest, Ewell was a royal manor. It was referred to in Domesday Book under the Copthorne Hundred as, 'Etwelle: King's land, two Mills'.[1] It had 48 villagers and four smallholders with 15 ploughs. The value before 1066 was put at £20 and it is interesting to note that Kingston, an important town where seven Saxon kings were crowned, was valued at £30, only £10 more than Ewell. Therefore, it seems that Ewell was a place of some consequence. Domesday Book makes no reference to a church at Ewell, but it does say that the church at Leret (Leatherhead) was attached to the manor with 40 acres of arable land valued at 20s. There is a passage to the effect that the 'men of the Hundred of Copthorne testify that two hides and one virgate were removed from this Manor. They were there in the time of King Edward but the reeves lent them to their friends'. This passage is believed to relate to Kingswood and it would appear that the land reverted to the Crown, since Kingswood was granted to Merton Priory by Henry II along with Ewell.

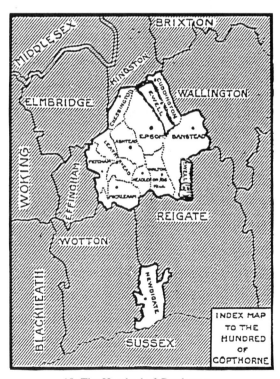

19. The Hundred of Copthorne

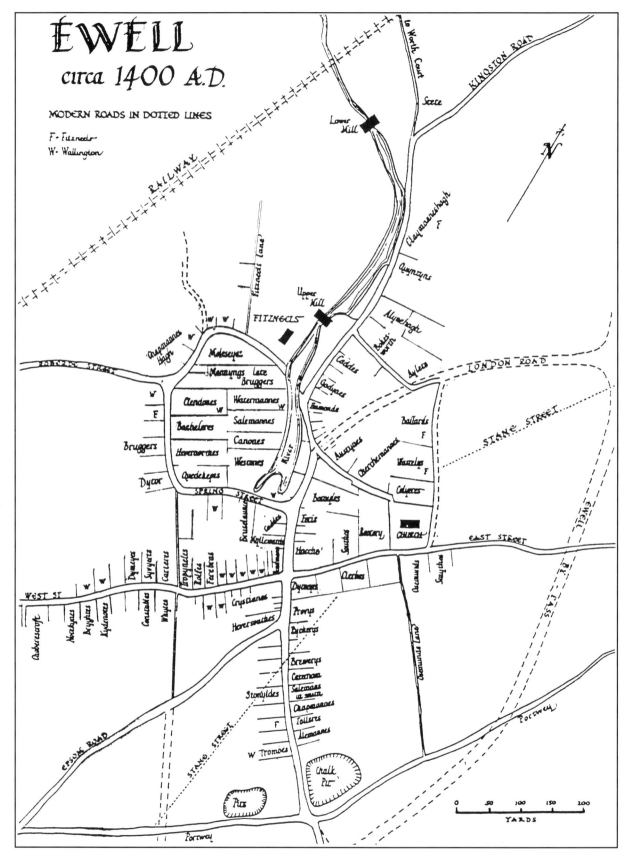

20. Ewell, *c.*1400: a conjectural map by C. A. F. Meekings/ P. Shearman.

Chapter 5

Medieval Ewell and the Manors

The Manorial Background

Life in medieval Ewell would have followed the general pattern of the feudal, manorial system. Apart from a small number of free tenants, the land was worked by villeins, small land-holders with perhaps as little as 10 or as much as 60 acres of land. They had to work for a certain number of days for the lord of the manor, and were not allowed to leave the manor without permission. A villein was also subject to numerous charges, such as an entry fee for his holding, when his daughter married or when his son went to school. On the villein's death the lord of the manor could also claim his best beast or chattel, while the church took second best, by a charge known as heriot.

Cottagers had a small cottage and a few acres and eked out an existence by helping villeins and working at times for the lord of the manor. The serfs were at the bottom of the heap, having no land and working virtually as slaves for the lord of the manor. The small-land holders who were freemen were in the minority. Not all the people worked on the land; for example there were the craftsmen, such as blacksmiths and carpenters and also masons, thatchers and tilers, many of whom moved around from village to village.

A villein in general lived in a small house in a village, with a small plot of land. The village was surrounded by open fields and common land, the fields being divided into strips a furlong long. Each man had a number of strips allocated in various parts of the open fields and often scattered over a wide area. The yield from the land was about a sixth of that of a comparable area today. He would also have rights of grazing on the common land. Some of the arable land was reserved for the lord of the manor and was worked by the villeins as part of their service. The manor was administered for the lord by his officials, stewards, bailiffs and reeves and business was settled in the manor court which all had to attend regularly. It can therefore be surmised that, working his own land with a heavy plough drawn by oxen or horses, working part of his time for the lord of the manor and paying a multitude of charges in cash or in kind, the peasant's life was arduous.

Life in Ewell in medieval times was dependent on two forces, the lord of the manor and the church. Ewell was a royal manor until 1158, when it was granted to Merton Priory and the priors became lords of the manor.[1] They remained so until the dissolution of Merton in 1538, although at times they assigned the lordship to others. For instance, Richard, tenth Earl of Arundel, who was executed as a traitor in 1398, held the manor at the time of his death. After the dissolution Ewell manor was leased to various people and then in 1563 Elizabeth I granted it to Henry, Earl of Arundel, and his heirs, for the sum of £885 12s. 10d. In 1730 the manor came into the hands of Lord John Russell, afterwards the Duke of Bedford, who sold it in 1755 to Edward Northey. The Northey family are still Lords of the Manor, the present lord (1992) being Martin Northey who lives at Swanage, but the title is now purely nominal.

The most illustrious of the family was Edward, 1652-1723: as most of the first sons were named Edward, one has to be careful about dates. This illustrious Northey was called to the bar in 1674, made Attorney General in 1701 and knighted in 1702. He was in office until 1707 and again from 1710 to 1718, so that he served during the reigns of William III, Anne and George I. He married Ann Jolliffe in 1687 and in 1696 acquired property in Epsom, where he had Woodcote House built. The present building is early 19th century. When the ex-Attorney General died in 1723 he was buried in a family vault in St Martin's church, Epsom. Some later members of the family are also in the vault, the most recent being Charlotte Northey, widow of the Rev. Edward Northey, who died in 1837. Later rebuilding of the chancel closed up the vault, and the Northeys had to acquire burial space in the churchyard.

It was the son of the Attorney General, Edward, 1691-1774, who became Lord of the Manor of Ewell and also of Cheam and Cuddington. Edward Richard Northey, 1794-1878, was deputy lieutenant for Surrey and its high sheriff in 1838. He gave Sir George Glyn £100 towards the construction of the new Ewell church in 1848 but professed little interest in Ewell and its activities. Major General Sir Edward Northey, 1868-1953, sold Woodcote House in 1939 and it has since been converted into flats.

The manor that was acquired by the Northeys was the main manor of Ewell. There were also three sub-manors, Fitznells, Batailles and Ruxley.

21. The Northeys became lords of the manor in 1755. The photograph on the left shows Major General Sir Edward Northey and Lady Northey at the time of the coronation of George VI in 1937.

22. Martin Northey, the present Lord of the Manor of Ewell, appears to be about to shave the Lord of the Manor of Epsom (the mayor, Councillor Lewis) in a barber's chair at Bourne Hall Museum, while Mrs. Northey assists. January 1991.

The Church

Although the manor of Ewell belonged to Merton Priory, the church was on land owned by Chertsey Abbey; it is not known when it was first built.[2] The building that was demolished when the new St Mary's church was built in 1847-8 had a 13th-century nave, although traces of 11th- and 12th-century work are said to have been found. In 1844 it was referred to as having a 'patched and unprepossessing exterior and having altogether been much maltreated'. The church was built largely of flint and consisted of the nave, south aisle, chancel and porch, with a tower at the west end. At the south-west corner was a chantry chapel built for Richard Bray in 1529; he died in 1559. The roof was tiled. The chancel was of a later date than the nave and had some good decorated period work, including a three-light east window. The 15th-century tower, which still stands, is of flint with stone dressing, and has an early 19th-century brick parapet curving up at the corners with staddle-stones on top. There is a wrought-iron weathervane made by a local smith, Richard Bliss, around 1789.

The nave and chancel were 93 ft. long and the width of the nave and aisle was 31 ft. In 1823 a gallery was erected, giving 153 seats in addition to the existing 422 seats. The church was clearly well attended: an observer in 1844 referred to the nave being choked with pews. The old church stood some 140 yards to the south of the present church.

23. The old church was largely of 13th-century construction with a 15th-century tower. In this view of the south side the chantry chapel built for Richard Bray in 1529 can be seen.

24. The old church that was demolished when St Mary's church was built in 1847-8. The tower was left standing to serve as a mortuary chapel. Some of the old stone was reused in the new church and other local buildings.

Initially Chertsey Abbey appointed the vicars, but in 1415 the advowson was given to the king in return for an annual pension of 20s. In the following year Henry V granted the church to the Prior and Convent of Newark and they retained it until the Dissolution.[3] After the Dissolution the advowson remained with the Crown until 1702, when it passed through several hands until it came by marriage into the Glyn family towards the middle of the 18th century. The Glyns controlled the church as patrons and the village as squires. In 1831 Sir George Lewen Glyn became Vicar and served for 50 years. The Glyn family continued as patrons of the church, though not as vicars, until the death of Margaret Glyn in 1946. The Bishop of Guildford is now the patron. Until the founding of the Diocese of Guildford in 1927 Ewell was in the Diocese of Winchester. Ewell gave its name to one of the four deaneries of Surrey, the others being Southwark, Guildford and Croydon.[4] This has been taken to imply that Ewell was a place of some importance when the deaneries were set up some time prior to 1291, the date of the first known reference to Ewell Deanery. There are also references in the Register of John de Pontissara, Bishop of Winchester, around 1300. In one of these the Dean is associated with the Archdeacon of Surrey in a mandate from the Bishop to bring to justice if possible 'certain sons of iniquity, whose names at present we know not, who on the first Saturday of the present Lent at Kasauton (Carshalton) laid violent hands on the Archdeacon's Official and the Dean of Ewell with two apparitors, the fear of God being laid aside, and wounded them with bloodshed. The Dean himself they threw into the water and nearly drowned him. ... They were to be solemnly excommunicated in the Churches on Sundays and Festivals, bells rung, and candles lighted'. The Ewell deanery existed until the reorganisation of rural deaneries in the 19th century. Further evidence of its importance is that in 1291 Ewell was valued for taxation purposes at £33 6s. 8d. and Kingston and Leatherhead were the only places in Surrey with a higher value. In comparative terms, Ewell was clearly more important in medieval times than during the last century. In 1853 Cardinal Newman wrote a letter in which he recalled a childhood coach trip to Brighton. He remarked 'I believe we changed coaches at Ewell. Is there such a place ?'

The Black Death

In medieval times an event that would have had a profound effect on Ewell, as in every town and village in the country, was the Black Death – no part of the kingdom escaped. The Great Pestilence struck in 1348 and in not much more than a year between 30 and 45 per cent of the total population perished. Men, women and children would be seized with violent pains in the chest, develop swellings, become delirious, vomit blood and die. Someone who was perfectly well in the morning could be dead by nightfall.

The most direct local reference to the Black Death is in the records of the Cuddington Court, which on 21 July 1349 reported the deaths of five freeholders and 15 villeins. The courts held in 1355-7 show that a number of families seem to have been completely wiped out, while some survivors held land formerly held by two or three tenants. Ewell must have suffered equally: the Fitznell records that will be referred to later show a substantial reduction in the number of inhabited houses on the rent roll, and arable land going out of cultivation. The social consequences of the Black Death were considerable and, in the years that followed, workers on the land and all types of craftsmen were scarce and they were able to demand more for their work. Laws were passed to regulate wages and conditions of work throughout the country, but they were impossible to enforce and there was some improvement in the living conditions of the working people.

Fitznell's Cartulary

An invaluable source of information on medieval Ewell is Fitznell's Cartulary, which is a copy of a collection of more than a hundred deeds relating to the purchase and exchange of properties throughout Ewell, Cuddington and Epsom from about 1200 to 1426. In medieval times the main preoccupation of landowners was playing Monopoly with their properties: they were for ever buying, exchanging or bequeathing. The complicated deeds that had to be drawn up must have made the fortunes of a number of lawyers. When landowners were not playing this Monopoly game they were prosecuting or defending lawsuits, which was also good for the lawyers.

25. The three-gabled portion of Fitznell's Manor House shown here in 1992, was originally built in the 17th century. Inside is a remnant of the house built in the 16th century. The right hand block was added at the beginning of the 19th century. In 1989 the building was restored and converted to offices.

26. The rear of Fitznell's Manor in 1992, within which is the solar of the manor house built by John Iwardeby early in the 16th century.

Many of the properties referred to in the deeds were granted for a lump sum plus a nominal rent, and one typical deed of about 1250 reads:

> William Pistor of Ewell to Gilbert of Ewell
> Grant for 8 shillings of ½ acre in Ewell Parish in Sorteforlang,
> To hold for a clove of gillyflower yearly at Christmas.

Another deed was worded — 'To hold for a pair of gloves or one penny yearly at Easter'.

The requirement to provide services to the Lord of the Manor went with the property, so such statements occur as 'To hold of the chief lords by due service'.

Fitznell's Manor was founded by a Mr. Robert, rector of Cuddington, who built up a small estate of strips in the open fields of Cuddington and Ewell and some property in Cuddington village. In about 1230 he handed it over to an orphaned nephew, Gilbert, who added to the lands and married Agnes, the sister of Walter of Basingstoke, another parson. Walter had been educated at Merton Priory and he changed his name to Merton. He rose to high office in both the church and state, and founded Merton College, Oxford, initially for the education of his nephews and other connections, including two of the children of Gilbert and Agnes of Ewell. In 1311 the estate passed into the hands of Sir Robert fitz Neil, from Buckinghamshire, who is believed to have married Agnes, daughter of Gilbert and Agnes, and the estate was subsequently known as Fitznells. A later heir suffered a head injury at a tournament which left him an idiot and the estate passed from the Fitznells, although it retained the name. In 1331 the Fitznell property in Ewell consisted of 250 acres of land, six acres of meadow and three water mills. In the 1430s the manor was acquired by John Iwardeby, an official in the lord treasurer's office, and passed on to his son John who died in 1525. It was he who, early in the 16th century, built the manor house, the solar wing of which survives in the building known as Fitznell's Manor. The present three-gabled block was added to the old solar wing in the early 17th century when the Horde family were in possession. In the second half of the 17th century the manor was conveyed to Thomas Turgis, one of the M.P.s of the Rotten Borough of Gatton.

There are memorial brasses relating to the Iwardebys and the Hordes in St Mary's church that were transferred from the old church. Lady Jane Iwardeby who died in 1519 is shown in the kennel head-dress of the period and the inscription includes 'Pray for me Lady Jane Iwarby sutyme wife of Sr John Iwarby of Ewell Knyght ... Lady helpe me and you'. Lady Dorothy Taylare, one time wife of Allen Horde, is shown with her five sons and five daughters, all Hordes. She died in 1577.

The Register

An important source of information on late medieval Ewell is the Register or Memorial of Ewell in 1408 which was drawn up for the lord of the manor, the Prior of Merton Priory. A copy of the original made in the first half of the 16th century was translated and edited by Cecil Deedes and published in 1913, together with a commentary. The introduction of the document says that it is a register of the customers and rents of the Manor of Ewell and goes on, 'And this Register is called a Memorial, in order that what is written therein may be more readily committed to human memory and that the property may not in future be claimed by other lords who hold lordships in the village and fraudulently taken away by evil men from the house and Church of Merton'. The register lists the hundreds of strips of an acre or half an acre that the fields were divided into, as well as the larger pieces of land. It also gives the rents and services that the holders had to provide. One William Aylet who held 13 acres had to pay 15d. per annum and perform many services for the lord of the manor including the following:

He shall work two days a week from the feast of St Michael to Easter from morning to noon and from Easter to the feast of St Michael to the third hour, and when the Autumn shall come he shall reap in each week one acre of corn. The same William shall mow and clear with his fellow workers a meadow which is called Kingsmead and shall carry the hay into the lord's grange and shall have for his labour by custom the third best sheep of the lord's fold and the third best cheese which he should not refuse. At the close of Autumn the same William shall carry the lord's manure from the court to the field with two carts a day from morning to noon. The same William shall wash and shear a hundred sheep of the lord with his fellows and shall have one loaf of the price of a halfpenny and cheese of the price of a farthing.

The same William has to do many other things, and finally: 'And if the same William shall have ten pigs or more the lord shall have the third best pig'. It is not clear when poor William was able to attend to his own thirteen acres.

Thirteen acres of land was a unit called a juger and some dozen other people held the same amount and were subject to similar duties. Two people held three jugers, but many more held less than one juger. However, it would seem that the duties set out were those that would have been in force before the Black Death and by 1408 very few of them would have been enforced.

Many of the strips referred to in the register were in the common field called Southfield, which extended from the village to the Downs and contained nearly 1,000 acres. It was not all arable land; about one third was woodland and copse. The Register gives information on the manor house in a passage which reads:

The site of the manor of Ewell contains two acres, one rood, in which is situated a hall with three chambers and a chapel, a kitchen, a dairy, a stable for the horses of the Bailiff, with one house of the attendant of the carriages, a stable for cart horses, a stable for pack horses, with a cow shed, an ox-shed, a piggery, a henhouse, a grange of corn, a grange of beans, a grange of oats, a dovecote. Also there is a watermill.

The Register makes reference to a total of 162 houses and crofts in the village.

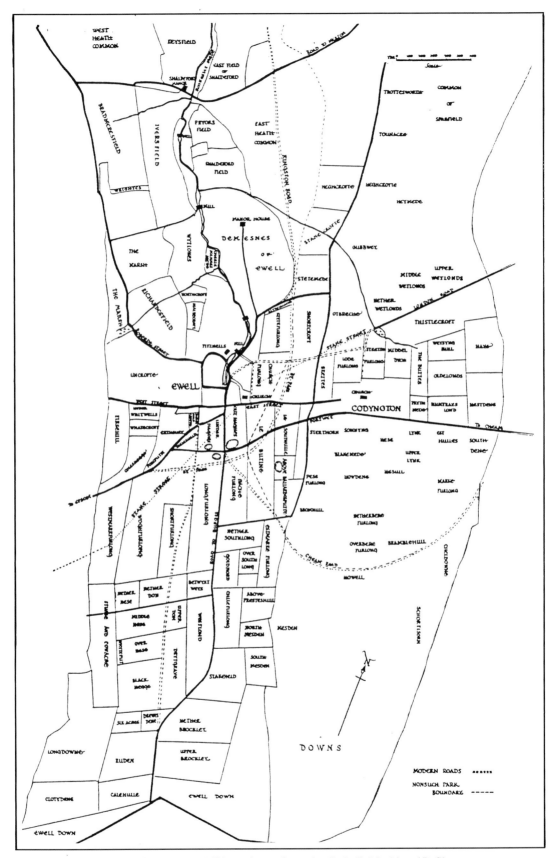

27. Ewell and Codyngton *c.*1400: conjectural map by C. A. F. Meekings/ P. Shearman

Ewell in 1400

C. A. F. Meekings and Philip Shearman drew up a map of Ewell Village round about 1400 based on information abstracted from the Cartulary and the Register. From the location and acreages of properties referred to and a certain amount of inspired guesswork they were able to produce a map and declare: 'The medieval street system is still there and most of the streets and lanes mentioned in the Register and Cartulary can be identified'.

The only building of medieval Ewell still standing is the tower of the old church. The centre of Ewell village was the crossroads formed by West Street, Church Street and High Street. In 1400 High Street was called Middle Street and Church Street was East Street. The manor house of the principal Manor of Ewell was known as Worth Court and stood north of the village. The last building of importance on the site was Ewell Court Farm, which was demolished *c.*1930. It was just south of the large house known as Ewell Court which was built in 1879.

The map on page 22 shows two mills: the lower mill was the Chertsey Abbey Mill, the upper mill belonged to Fitznell's and was working as recently as 1952. There was a third mill at Worth Court. The 18th-century upper mill was recently restored and converted to offices, although it would be more accurate to say that it was rebuilt and consequently it is no longer a listed building. The house of the upper mill no longer stands, which is the opposite of the situation at the lower mill. The Lower Mill House, which is largely an early 18th-century construction, is still there, but the mill itself was destroyed by fire in June 1938. For some years in the 18th century the lower mill made paper.

Although much of the Ewell parish of 1400 has been built over, some open spaces remain. There are still smallholdings at North Looe, on what was the Southfield, and between North Looe and Ewell there is grassland. There is still some open land north of the village, along the Hogsmill, which is open to the public, but it is not the old common land. The three commons were separated by properties along the Hogsmill held by various landowners and areas of these properties form the present-day public land. The commons have been built on: the Marsh is under West Ewell; West Heath is now Ruxley; East Heath was in the area of Auriol and Ewell Court Wards.

28. The Upper Mill in Kingston Road seen here in 1929, was built in the 18th century. Around 1984 it was so thoroughly 'restored' that it is no longer a listed building.

29. The Upper Mill in 1990 after it had been restored/rebuilt.

30. A miller dresses a mill stone in the Upper Mill in the 1920s.

31. The Lower Mill and the Mill House, in Kingston Road, *c*.1873. The grandparents of Mr. Richard Henderson, the last miller of Ewell (at the Upper Mill) can be seen with some of their children.

32. The Lower Mill House, in Kingston Road, is a restored 17th/18th-century building now used as offices, photographed in 1992.

The Manor of Batailles

We have spoken of Fitznell's Manor. Another of the three subordinate manors of Ewell was Batailles, which took its name from the first owner, William de Bataille, who was granted it by Henry I at the beginning of the 12th century. The lands of the manor were mostly scattered in the arable furlongs but with some enclosures just north of the village. The family also held land in Cuddington. The manor house lay on the north eastern outskirts of the village on a site within the grounds of the present Glyn House.

After going through various hands, Batailles passed by marriage to the Saunder family. The first Saunder to hold the manor in his own right was Henry, who inherited part of the estate in 1470 and purchased the other parts.[5] In 1408 the island site on which Bourne Hall stands was divided into about a dozen properties, only a few of which belonged to the Batailles estate, but by 1577 nearly all the land now forming Bourne Hall grounds had been acquired by the Saunder family and a mansion had been built. It was described, in a survey of that year, as a fair mansion house with a gatehouse, a forecourt, hall, parlour and other edifices and buildings with two backyards, stables and barns, also a dove house, two gardens and an orchard. Excavations have indicated that it stood to the east of Bourne Hall.

It is thought that the mansion was built by Henry Saunder towards the end of the 15th century. In 1577 Nicholas Saunder was the owner. As a Catholic at the time of Elizabeth I, he suffered for his beliefs and spent some time in the Fleet Prison. He died in 1587. Five generations of the Saunder family possessed Batailles Manor before it was sold to Thomas Turgis in 1659. It is probable that the sale was made necessary by Sir Nicholas Saunder, the son of the previous Nicholas, losing money from a scheme to convey water from Hoddesdon in Hertfordshire to London in a covered aqueduct. It was in competition with the more successful New River scheme and had to be abandoned.

Ruxley Manor

The third subordinate manor was Ruxley. This had originally been called Shawford, that being the name of its first owner back in the 12th century. The name had many transformations, including Saldeford, Scaldeford and Shaldeford, and in *c*.1480 the name was changed to Rokesley, the name of the then owner, and finished up as Ruxley.

In 1577 the manor lands consisted of at least 120 acres on the north of Ewell, plus some property in the village. The old manor house of Shawford stood on the left bank of the Hogsmill close to the ford where Ruxley Lane is now. The various owners of the manor were involved in the customary lawsuits, one of which in the 13th century was dependent on the legitimacy of the children of Gerard de Shawford. According to the court records, 'Gerard had loved a girl named Maud, so that he had intercourse with her, and had by her first John, then Peter and lastly Agnes. But when Maud should have been purified, the church refused to accord her its rites unless she would abjure Gerard and Gerard abjure her or else marry her. Gerard would not abjure her and instead straightway married her and afterwards had by her one William'. The court decided that William was the rightful heir.

In 1659 part of Ruxley Manor was sold to Thomas Turgis, who later bought the remainder and acquired all three of the Ewell sub-manors, Fitznell's, Batailles and Ruxley. They then passed through other hands and in 1784 all three were sold to Thomas Calverley, who died in 1797 and left them to his son Thomas.

33. Ruxley Splash seen here in 1915, was the ford where Ruxley Lane crossed the Hogsmill River.

Kingswood

Kingswood was originally part of the Ewell Manor that was granted to Merton Priory. After the Dissolution Henry VIII annexed Kingswood to the Honour of Hampton Court. Queen Elizabeth granted it to Lord Howard of Effingham, but it subsequently passed through other hands as an independent manor. However, Kingswood remained part of the parish of Ewell until 1838 when a new parish was formed with a portion of Banstead.

According to the deed of endowment of the Vicarage of Ewell in 1458 there was a chapel at Kingswood, but the Vicar of Ewell was not obliged to celebrate mass there. It was also laid down that the people of Kingswood should be buried at Ewell, the body being met at Provost's Cross by the Vicar of Ewell 'as had been the custom from ancient times' — the custom resulted from an order by the Prior of Newark Convent. Provost's Cross seems to have been the junction of Cheam Road and Mongers Lane, where Thomas Provys held the chalk pit to the north. In March 1783 the Ewell Vestry agreed that the poor of the hamlet of Kingswood would be received into the Ewell workhouse, provided that 'no woman Big with Bastard Child shall be sent to the workhouse until one month after the Delivery of the Bastard Child'.

Consideration of the manors of Ewell has taken us through the medieval period, for most of which the lordship of the main manor was held by Merton Priory, and much of the parish was divided between the three sub-manors. Furthermore, the church was built on land belonging to Chertsey Abbey, which held the advowson, and so the unifying influence of a resident lord of the manor with a close relationship with the church was lacking.

Chapter 6

Tudor Ewell and the Palace of Nonsuch

The Palace of Nonsuch

The major event of Tudor Ewell was the building of Nonsuch Palace in the neighbouring parish of Cuddington, and the enclosure of land that had been tilled for centuries to form the Great and Little Parks. The enclosure extended beyond the area of Cuddington Parish and took in more than 150 acres of Ewell.

Henry VIII had plans for a great hunting estate based on Hampton Court and extending as far south as Epsom. It involved the rebuilding of the medieval palace of Oatlands at Weybridge and the construction of a new palace at Cuddington to provide hunting lodges. The new palace was to show the world his wealth and grandeur and put him one up in the vainglory contest with Francis I: it was to be called Nonsuch. There was plenty of loot from the monasteries to provide the resources and 'there emerged a building of unrivalled splendour, lavishly decorated to the point of vulgarity, a monument to princely ostentation' (John Dent). Richard Codington, the Lord of the Manor, was offered the manor of Ixworth in Suffolk in exchange for Cuddington, an offer it would not have been wise to refuse.

Henry chose a spot on slightly rising ground with extensive views as the site of the new palace. The fact that it was occupied by St Mary's church and graveyard was no obstacle: the building was demolished and foundation trenches and sewers were driven through the graves. Tons of stone from Merton Priory, much of it finely carved, went into the foundations of the new palace. The demolition of the Priory started even before the surrender document was signed. The building of the palace started in April 1538, some six months before completion of the legal formalities for the acquisition of Cuddington.

34. The south front of Nonsuch Palace from an 1837 engraving by George Hollis. The engraving was based on a 1582 engraving by Joris Hoefnagel which had been based on his drawing of 1568.

35. An imaginative reconstruction of the south west corner of Nonsuch Palace and its gardens that appeared in *The Builder* in 1894.

Nonsuch Palace has been referred to as the most remarkable of all Tudor buildings. It was built around two courtyards, an outward court to the north with accommodation for court officers and minor visitors, and an inner court to the south around which were the royal apartments. The approach from the London Road entered the Outward Court. The buildings around the Inner Court were three storeys high; the south front of the palace was flanked by towers five-storeys high and was 200 ft. long. The inward and outward facing walls of the buildings of the Inner Court were covered with moulded plaster panels with classical motifs, surrounded by frames of carved slate, much of the decoration being gilded. There were statues and fountains. The palace was surrounded by ornamental grounds, with knot gardens, a maze and orchards, shady walks and more statues and fountains; no 'state of the art' feature of Tudor gardening was omitted. An elaborate Banqueting House was built on a large plinth some quarter of a mile from the palace.

Paul Hentzner, a German traveller who saw Nonsuch in 1598, gave the following account:

Nonesuch a royal retreat, in a place formerly called Cuddington, a very healthful situation, chosen by King Henry VIII for his pleasure and retirement, and built by him with an excess of magnificence and elegance, even to ostentation: one would imagine everything that architecture can perform to have been employed in this one work. There are everywhere so many statues that seem to breathe, so many miracles of consummate art, so many casts that rival even the perfection of Roman antiquity, that it may well claim and justify its name of Nonesuch.

The Palace itself is so encompassed with parks full of deer, delicious gardens, groves ornamented with trellis work, cabinets of verdure and walks so embrowned with trees, that it seems to be a place pitched upon by Pleasure herself, to dwell in along with Health. In the pleasure and artificial gardens are many columns and pyramids of marble, two fountains that spout water one round the other like a pyramid, upon which are perched small birds that stream water out of their bills. In the grove of Diana is a very agreeable fountain, with Actaeon turned into a stag, as he was sprinkled by the goddess and her nymphs, with inscriptions.

Henry did not have much opportunity to enjoy his grandiose new hunting lodge. When he died in 1547 it was unfinished, although largely complete: it is doubtful whether he made use of it on more than three occasions. Edward VI and his successor, Queen Mary, showed little interest in Nonsuch and in 1556 Mary sold the Palace and Little Park to Henry Fitzalan, 12th Earl of Arundel. When Elizabeth came to the throne in 1558, the widowed Arundel had hopes of becoming her consort. The completion of Nonsuch was hurried along so that Elizabeth could be invited to a magnificent and extravagant house-warming in 1559.

The Earl's matrimonial plans came to nothing, and in 1571 he was arrested for being involved in a plot against Elizabeth. He spent some time in confinement, partly at Nonsuch and died in 1579 with enormous debts to the Crown, leaving Nonsuch to his son-in-law, Lord

Lumley. Elizabeth was entertained at Nonsuch by Lumley, and in 1592 he gave her the palace in settlement of his debts. He became Keeper in what had been his own house and continued to live there as before. The Queen began spending money on the building and the court met there frequently. The reign of Elizabeth was the heyday of Nonsuch.

James I settled Nonsuch on the Queen, Anne of Denmark, and the royal family made some use of the palace. Charles I came to the throne in 1625 and in 1627 he granted Nonsuch to Henrietta Maria. The execution of Charles on 30 January 1649 marked the end of Nonsuch as a royal palace.

The victorious Parliamentarians confiscated all property belonging to the royal family and in 1654 the Palace and Little Park were conveyed to John Lambert, Major General of all the forces in England and Scotland. When Charles II came back in 1660 following the Restoration the Palace and both parks were restored to Henrietta Maria. She died in 1669 and in 1671 the palace and parks were granted to trustees on behalf of the 31-year-old Barbara, Countess of Castlemaine, who had been made Baroness of Nonsuch, Countess of Southampton and Duchess of Cleveland. Officially these honours were granted in recognition of the services of her father, the late Viscount Grandison: unofficially they were a reward for Barbara's more intimate services to Charles. Barbara Castlemaine had no interest in Nonsuch and, so far as is known, never visited it. She had an extravagant lifestyle, which included gambling, and in spite of an enormous income granted by the King was always short of money. In 1682 she persuaded Charles II to sign a warrant allowing the palace to be pulled down and the materials sold off, because it was in such a bad state of repair. Demolition started shortly after and proceeded in stages.

36. Nonsuch Palace from the north east from a painting by Hendrick Danckert, *c*.1660; for a long time it was wrongly considered to be a view of St James' Palace.

37. Nonsuch Mansion in Nonsuch Park was built by Jeffrey Wyatt (later Sir Jeffrey Wyattville) in 1802-6 for Samuel Farmer. Visitors to the area are known to have mistaken the Mansion for the Palace of Nonsuch which was demolished in the 17th century.

38. The excavations on the site of Nonsuch Palace in 1959 were probably the largest archaeological dig to be carried out in this country in one season. John Dent, then Chief Librarian for Epsom and Ewell, who played a large part in organising the project, is shown with a party of visitors at the end of a tour.

39. The site of Nonsuch Palace is marked only by three stone obelisks. The palace was demolished in the 17th century after Charles II gave it to Barbara Castlemaine.

When Barbara Castlemaine died in 1709 it was a mortgaged Nonsuch estate that was inherited by her grandson Charles, 2nd Duke of Grafton. In 1731 the Grafton estates in Surrey were sold off, the Little Park and the Great Park, by then known as Worcester Park, going to separate purchasers. Joseph Thompson bought the Little Park and it is believed that part of the house he had built survives in the kitchen wing of Nonsuch Mansion. The estate then passed to the Whateley family who were responsible for the development of the gardens around Nonsuch Mansion. In the 19th century, when the Farmer family were the owners, the gardens became famous throughout the country. During the Whateley period, the remnants of the palace were levelled off and turfed over; a tree-lined road was made through the centre of the site. Nonsuch Palace was erased from the landscape and from then on existed only in historic records and a few paintings and drawings. The foundations of Nonsuch slumbered under the turf, their precise whereabouts a matter of conjecture, until 1959. The site of the palace could well have been built over in the same way that the Great Park disappeared under Worcester Park and Stoneleigh. Fortunately, as building work began to encroach on the Little Park, it was realised what a shame it would be to lose such a beautiful historic area, and a movement was started to preserve what remained. The Epsom and Ewell Urban District Council, the Sutton and Cheam Borough Council, the Surrey County Council and the London County Council banded together and in 1937 bought the park for the public. It is now managed by the Nonsuch Park Joint Management Committee consisting of members from both the Epsom and Ewell Borough Council and the London Borough of Sutton.

Martin Biddle, an archaeological consultant to the Ministry of Works, became interested in excavating Nonsuch Palace and was able to gain the support of the Ministry. After discussions with people likely to be interested, a Nonsuch Palace Excavation Committee was set up. One of the members was John Dent, Borough Librarian of Epsom and Ewell, who for several years had been collecting copies of all the books, manuscripts and pictures he could find relating to the palace. He was able to make a major contribution to planning and organising the excavation that started in July 1959 and went on for 12 weeks.

The Nonsuch Palace excavation was probably the largest archaeological excavation ever carried out in a single year in this country: all the foundations of the building were exposed and the cellars were dug out. Under the palace the remains of Cuddington Church were found, including some burials. In the summer of 1959 the work generated tremendous interest. It was featured on television, and during the 12 weeks it attracted around 60,000 visitors, whose contributions helped to fund the digging. There was no difficulty in obtaining sufficient volunteer diggers.[1] The vast quantities of artefacts and fragments of building materials unearthed enabled many of the questions about the structure to be answered. In his book, *The Quest for Nonsuch*, John Dent gave a full account of the building of the palace, its decline and obliteration, and its rediscovery.

The building of Nonsuch would have had a significant effect on Ewell. During the nine years or so of the initial phase of the construction it would have generated business for the inns and alehouses and employment for the men of the village. The accounts of the building of the Palace show that in September 1538 more than 500 men were employed, including 200 labourers. Richard Bray of Ewell supplied some of the timber. Ewell Manor, along with many others, became part of the Honour of Hampton Court which was established in 1539 and which was essentially a hunting estate comparable to the New Forest.

Having a royal palace as a close neighbour would have brought opportunities for employment when the court was in residence and work for the local tradespeople. Tradition has it that Maids of Honour lodged in Church Street, Ewell.

On the completion of the 1959 excavations, earth-moving equipment moved in and the 6,000 tons of excavated earth and rubble were tipped and pushed back and the site levelled off and turfed. The foundations of the unique palace, of which it could truly be said there was none such other, have disappeared and the site is marked only by three stone obelisks about four ft. high which indicate the lengths of the two courts.

Ewell at the time of Elizabeth I

A useful account of Ewell in the middle of the reign of Elizabeth I is provided by the Survey of the Parish of Ewell taken in 1577 by Thomas Taylor, Surveyor of Surrey. The survey gives detailed information on the land holdings in the village, the great common field of Southfield, the Common Downs and the land to the north of the village which included the three commons of Eastheath, Westheath and the Marsh. Reference is made to 63 dwellings.

The biggest landowner was Nicholas Saunder, who held about 340 acres. Nicholas had 250 acres in the Common Field and 77 acres in enclosed fields, as well as the properties in the village already mentioned. The next biggest landowner was Elizabeth Horde of Fitznell's with 252 acres. The major change in roads between 1400 and 1577 was the result of the building of Nonsuch Palace and the enclosing of the Great and Little Parks: in 1400 Church Street (then East Street) continued eastwards to Cuddington and Cheam. The building of the Palace cut the road more or less where the by-pass is now and a new road had to be made skirting the southern boundary of the Little Park. The original road still exists in parts as Vicarage Lane and the Avenue across the Park to Cheam. The name West Street had been changed to Gallowstrete: tradition has it that gallows had been erected there. Fortunately, or unfortunately, depending on one's viewpoint, the gallows are no longer there and the name has reverted to West Street.

In 1577 Spring Street was called Beggars Rowe and Chessington Road, Robertstretelane. At the crossroads where there was once a cross stood the townhouse which Taylor described as, 'Here in the strete is situate and standing a house late builded which is called the Townehouse not letten but put to the use of the Towne onely'. The townhouse was pulled down in the latter half of the 18th century but the junction of High Street, Church Street and West Street still remains the centre of Ewell Village. The building is thought to have been on the corner, just in front of the Market House Stores. The jettied part of these houses has been dated as mid-16th century and they could well be houses referred to by Thomas Taylor in the 1577 survey.

Across the road where West Street goes off is the house popularly known as Maldwyns, a 17th-century building with a front of mathematical tiles added in the following century. 17 High Street, on the corner of Church Street, is considered to be largely early 17th century.

In 1577, 9 High Street was the *Red Lyon* inn, the earliest known hostelry in Ewell. The name was later changed to the *Queen Anne*, and again changed in *c.*1760, to the *Queen's Head*, but by 1835, it had ceased to trade as a public house. Cloudesley Willis lived at No. 9 and referred to it as 'preserving behind its formal early 19th-century front, one of the most ancient structures in Ewell'. The building at the corner of Cheam Road and the High Street is considered to be basically late 16th century and so would have been built soon after Taylor's survey.

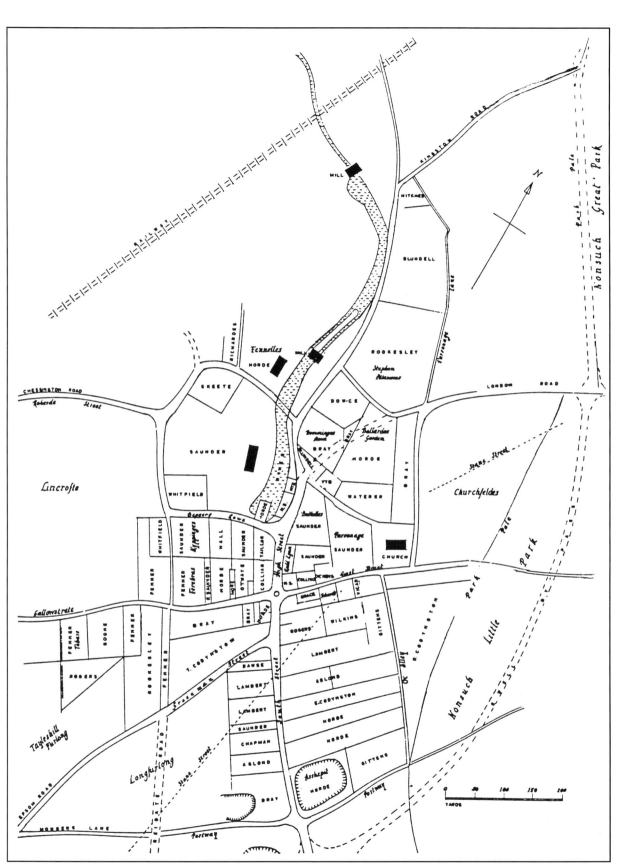

40. Ewell in 1577: conjectural map by P. Shearman

41. The corner of High Street and Church Street, 1992. The jettied part of the buildings dates from around 1550 and the remainder from around 1600.

42. Church Street from the end of West Street in 1992. Until 1834 the London to Epsom traffic used Church Street.

43. The corner of High Street and West Street, a 17th-century building with a front of mathematical tiles added in the 18th century.

44. The building on the left is 9 High Street, where Cloudesley Willis lived. It incorporates an early 16th-century building that was once an inn.

45. High Street (Green Man Street) in 1830 as seen from the first floor of the *Bull's Head* Inn by Edward Hassell, son of John Hassell.

46. An 1825 watercolour by John Hassell, of the *Bull's Head* Inn which stood at the junction of Cheam Road with High Street. It was pulled down in the 1860s and the Midland Bank now occupies the site.

Chapter 7

The Mid-17th Century

The Battle of Ox Lane

I must confess that the title, 'The Battle of Ox Lane' was written tongue in cheek. In his excellent *Quest for Nonsuch* John Dent states that there was a fierce engagement between Roundheads and Cavaliers in which many were killed, in 'a pass between Ewell and Nonsuch Park which is believed to be the footpath which is today known as Ox Lane'. However, contemporary accounts lead to the conclusion that the main encounter was near Kingston and the engagement near Ewell was only a skirmish.[1] Nonetheless, the incident, which some refer to as one of the last battles of the civil war, and others refer to as a Royalist uprising after the war had ended, had elements of drama, and is worth relating.

Charles I had been captured and the Civil War was essentially over, but there was considerable unrest because of heavy taxation, high prices and restrictions on freedom. There was also much resentment over the billeting of soldiers throughout the county at the householders' expense. The Earl of Holland thought the time was ripe for an uprising, and supported by other nobles, including the Duke of Buckingham, the Duke's younger brother Lord Francis Villiers and the Earl of Peterborough, gathered together a force of some five or six hundred troops, both foot and horse, at Kingston at the beginning of July 1648. On 6 July they began marching first to Dorking and then on to Reigate. It would seem that the Earl of Holland expected the country people to rise up and join him, and when this did not happen, having no alternative plan, he began to lead the Royalist troops back to Kingston. They were overtaken on the outskirts of Ewell by a Roundhead advance guard of Sir Michael Livesey's forces and shots were exchanged, followed by a fiercer encounter near Nonsuch Palace.

The Cavaliers turned and formed up in a defensive position on rising ground on what was Kingston Common, about a mile south east of where Surbiton Station is now. There was then a curious interlude in which individual troopers came out of the opposing ranks and fought each other as in a medieval tournament. This was ended when the Roundhead cavalry charged and the Cavaliers withdrew, still fighting, to Kingston.

The 19-year-old Lord Francis Villiers, whose horse was killed in the retreat, fought with his back to a tree until a Roundhead reached round from behind, struck off his steel cap and wounded him in the head. He was then slain. The Roundheads drew up on the outskirts of Kingston to await reinforcements, thinking to attack in the morning, only to find when they entered the town that the enemy had slipped away. Holland was later captured and executed; Buckingham and Peterborough escaped abroad. (Lord Francis Villiers was a cousin of Barbara Villiers, later Countess Castlemaine, who was responsible for the demolition of Nonsuch Palace.)

An account of the engagement by Major Lewis Audeley of Livesey's Horse, published in a Parliamentary paper on 8 July 1648, claimed that about 20 Cavaliers were slain and about one hundred captured.

The Hearth Tax

Charles II returned in 1660 at the Restoration, and two years later Parliament passed an Act 'for establishing an additional Revenue upon his Majestie, his heires and successors, for the better support of his and their Crown and dignity'. Under the act the occupier of every house in the kingdom had to pay two shillings a year on every chimney hearth, unless they were exempted by poverty. Industrial hearths were also exempt.

Records of the application of the tax in Ewell in 1664 have survived and provide information on who lived in the parish at that time and in what sort of style. There were 74 chargeable house occupiers who were responsible for 262 hearths. The highest assessment, 13 hearths, was for Timothy Cutler, whose house was in Church Street. Widow Peirce, and several other people, had only one hearth. The Act remained in force until 1689.

Chapter 8

Administration and the Poor

The Vestry

In medieval times local affairs and justice were dealt with by the manorial court, presided over by a representative of the lord of the manor. However, people would meet in the vestry of the parish church to discuss problems and eventually by the 17th century Parliament made these vestry meetings responsible for matters such as the upkeep of local roads and bridges and the care of the poor and orphans as required by the Poor Laws.

The Ewell Vestry met at least four times a year and the wide range of matters they discussed is revealed by the minutes of these meetings. One of the most important jobs of the vestry was the appointment of parish officers, including Constables, Waywardens, Overseers of the Poor, Churchwardens and Beadles. The Vestry was also responsible for setting the rates and arranging for their collection.

Keeping the peace was the concern of the Vestry and at a meeting on 23 April 1807 there was a complaint 'that several boys belonging to the Parish behave in a Riotous Manner in several parts of the Town and on Sundays in Particular'. It was recommended that 'the Constables and other Parish Officers will endeavour all they can to suppress such behaviour in future'. In 1853 the Commissioners of Police were requested 'to establish a Police Station in some central position in the Town of Ewell as under the present arrangements of the men living in private houses there is great difficulty and delay in procuring the aid of a policeman in sudden emergencies'. The request was not accepted, and to this day Ewell does not have a police station.

Pest control was also the responsibility of the Vestry, and on 1 May 1828 it was resolved that in future the Church Wardens would pay two pence per dozen for sparrows.[1]

Rowdy bell ringers were sometimes a problem and on 25 June 1857, 'It was Resolved that the Vicar and Churchwardens be requested to take such measures as in their judgement may be deemed necessary for organising the Bellringers and for bringing them under proper control'. It led to the drafting of, 'Rules to be observed by the Company of Ringers' in August 1857. The object was to give the Vicar and Churchwardens control of bell ringing, and included the provision that the bells could be rung only with their permission. Drinking and smoking in the belfry were subject to a fine of sixpence, and swearing and bad language twopence. Bell ringers probably considered that the importance of their services merited a degree of independence. In the belfry of St Mary's is the legend: 'We to the Church the living call, and to the Grave do summon all'.

The arrival of the railways brought arguments with the railway companies over fair rates reflected in a minute of 11 January 1849 that 'Mr Hall, on behalf of the Brighton and S.C. Railway Company do protest against the assessment of the Company and inquired on what principle the assessment was made'. The matter required the setting up of a committee and reference to the Quarter Sessions, before a settlement was reached in 1851 whereby a rateable value of £300 covering the line, land under cultivation and the station was agreed.

The Vestry took an interest in the provision of amenities, and on the 27 October 1807 'It was agreed that a Lamp should be erected opposite the *King's Head* and that Thomas Goldsmith shall receive One Guinea Per Year for finding Oil and lighting the same'.

Discussions in July 1861 suggest that there had been problems in the provision of main drainage, since 'In the opinion of this meeting it is highly desirable that all persons now draining into the main sewer should take measures for preventing the flow of sewage and other offensive matters into it and revert to the former system of having cesspools on their premises'.

The Ewell Parish Vestry could not be said to have been a very democratic institution: only the more important members of the community took part in the meetings, and if it came to a vote, occupiers of highly rated properties were allowed more than one vote. The powers of the Vestry were brought to an end in 1894 when an Act was passed to set up urban and rural district councils.

At their last meeting in May 1894, matters relating to the setting up of the rural district council were discussed, including the following proposals: (a) The parish should be grouped with neighbouring parishes. The answer was No. (b) The parish should be divided into wards. The answer was No. (c) Should a joint scheme for drainage work with Cheam and Cuddington as advised necessary by the Epsom Rural Sanitary Authority be accepted. The answer was No. It was considered to be too expensive.

The Rural District Council

When the Ewell Rural District Council was set up in 1894 it met in an upstairs room in the High Street. The Council lasted until 1933 when Ewell was merged with Epsom to form the Urban District of Epsom and Ewell, which became a borough in 1937.

The Rural District Council was very much concerned with the minutiae of local affairs, as their minutes reveal. In November 1909 arrangements were made for the collection of house refuse every two weeks. It was not until 1923 that weekly collections were made.

Cloudesley Willis who was Secretary of the Ewell Liberal and Labour Association complained about the lack of adequate housing for working people. In 1911 there were 357 cottages let at rents from ten shillings down to five shillings per week, 96 let at five shillings down to four shillings and 11 under this price. The normal labourer's wage was well under 18s. per week, so it would seem that rent was a major item of his budget.

Minutes of meetings during the First World War reflect the impact of that conflict with its insatiable demands for manpower on a local community. As early as December 1914, 159 people from Ewell had enlisted, and there are frequent references to those killed and wounded and to those receiving decorations for gallantry. During the war air raids were a threat to the extent that plans had to be drawn up for extinguishing lights during raids. Discharged Belgian soldiers had been housed in the large house, Ewell Grove, and on 10 May 1915 an appeal was made that people should not treat them to drinks. In July 1917 it was agreed to congratulate General Northey on his success with his troops in East Africa against the Germans, in view of the long and close relationship of generations of Northeys with the people of Ewell. In July 1918 arrangements were made for collecting fruit stones and nut shells for making charcoal as a protection against poison gas.

47. James Chuter Ede had a distinguished career in local and national government, which included being the first mayor of Epsom and Ewell, Chairman of Surrey County Council and Home Secretary in the 1945-51 Labour Government. He was elevated to the peerage as Baron Chuter-Ede in 1964 and died in Ewell in 1965 at the age of 83.

However, in spite of the war, normal life had to go on, and on 12 October 1914 a complaint was considered that Mr. Bell had turned out his horse into the recreation ground without permission or payment to the Council. On 14 February 1916 an apology from a police constable for riding his bicycle on the footpath was accepted. The war came to an end after four and a quarter years on 11 November 1918, and the Rural District Council was once more able to concentrate on purely local affairs.

In July 1923 the Council recommended that neither the horses nor the motor for the fire engine should be used when the brigade was summoned to a fire within 300 yards of the fire station, but that the manual engine should be hauled by manpower.

As early as 1907 cars were becoming a cause for concern. A letter was written to the County Council protesting against the use of the roads by motorists to the detriment of the general public, and asking what steps could be taken to enable the public to use the roads again with comfort and safety. A further letter provided the information that a 'racing motor car was seen on the Kingston Road at the top of Beggars Hill travelling between 40 and 50 miles an hour; it was a great wonder no-one was killed'.

In 1923 the main grievances against motor traffic were the dazzling lights, objectionable smoke, speeding and noise, and the danger to passengers on the top of omnibuses passing under Kingston Road railway bridge. It was suggested that signs would be needed on the bridge warning bus passengers to duck.

48. Ewell High Street in about 1910. The upper bay window on the left is where the Rural District Council met until 1933 when Ewell and Epsom were merged. The fire engine was kept down below.

In 1922 consideration was being given to setting up a local museum, and in 1923 Messrs. Knight, Frank and Rutley wrote offering to sell Ewell Castle as a museum. The offer was not accepted, and Ewell had to wait until 1970 for the Epsom and Ewell Museum.

In February 1926 Mr A. E. Wiltshire, a well-known local man, was killed crossing the railway at the end of West Street, and this led to the erection of a footbridge.

The Poor of Ewell

Although Ewell was a prosperous village, particularly in the 19th century, not all the villagers were free from poverty, and the well-being of some was very much dependent on the operation of the Poor Laws. The numerous acts passed by successive governments had a profound effect on the way in which parishes dealt with their poor. The implementation of the Poor Laws was a major function of the Parish Vestry.

It is not known when Ewell first had a workhouse. The first known reference is in the Overseers' Accounts for March 1760, when it appears to have been part of the Pest House, an early form of isolation hospital. The workhouse was sometimes called the Alms House, and that is probably a more apt description of it at that time.

It was not until 1781 that action was taken regarding a workhouse proper by forming a committee to consider 'The setting up of a Poor House for the reception of the Poor and a proper person to look after the said Poor'. In May of that year an estimate by Mr. Henry Kitchen for building and furnishing a new wing of the old Pest House was accepted. It was a very comprehensive estimate and went down to such details as three tablecloths, six towels, two water pails, three wash tubs, chamber pots, a pair of bellows, mops, brooms, brushes and sundry other articles. The total cost of the building work, furniture and utensils was £98 8s. 0d.

In July 1781:
> John Bulley and Mary his wife were Elected by a great Majority of Parishioners to Superintend the Workhouse for twelve months certain if he gives satisfaction to the Churchwardens and Overseers and a Committee which is to be appointed, at the Sum of Six Guineas a Quarter. He, the said John Bulley and Mary his wife, engages in consideration of the Sum before Mentioned to keep the Poor of the said Parish in constant employ at Spinning, Knitting and other Work that will be most Advantagious and likewise distribute the quantity of food in a proper and judicious manner and also to keep them Clean and decent and to instruct the Children in Reading. The said John Bulley and Mary his wife to have their Board, Lodging, firing and candles in common with the said Poor found him, and also the stipulated Sum above.

In October 1781:
> It was Resolved and Agreed that the following Allowances of Provisions should be distributed to each person Residing in the Workhouse by John Bulley and Mary his wife. Discretionally as follows:-
> On Sunday Fresh Meat for Dinner
> Monday Bread and 2 oz. of Cheese each Person for Dinner
> Tuesday Bread and 2 oz. Meat each Person for Dinner
> Wednesday Suet Pudding each Person for Dinner
> Thursday Meat
> Friday Meat
> Saturday Soop.
> For Breakfasting every day Water gruel, Broth or Porridge, or one ounce of Butter.
> For Suppers one ounce of Butter or two Ounces of Cheese.
> Two pints of Beer and one Pound of Bread each Person every day.
> Three Bushels of Coal and one pound of Candles to be allowed every week.

There was a new agreement with John Bulley in 1784 whereby he received £290 a year, out of which he fed the Workhouse inmates. After his death in 1789 there appeared to be problems in keeping a Workhouse Master and there were frequent changes. The number of people in the Workhouse was usually around 25, although there were 34 in 1816.

The main employment was the carding and spinning of wool, and in 1786 it was minuted that certain inmates, eleven men and eight women, 'shall be ordered to keep to work by the Contractor of the House so as to Card and Spin Eighteen Pounds per day. And if any of the said Poor shall refuse to work or idle away their time that a Complaint shall be immediately made to the Magistrate, Churchwardens or Overseers by the said Contractor or Inspector'.

The spun wool was sold and helped defray some of the expenses. This activity seems to have been discontinued by 1816 as references to it no longer appear in the Overseers Accounts. There are, however, more references to outdoor work and an entry in 1819 refers to fruit, vegetables and roasting pigs being sold to the value of £36 2s. 0d.

The 1802 the Enclosure Award map showed the Workhouse as two buildings in a small plot of land at the far end of West Street, and the Poor House cottages a little to the north.

In 1826 the Poor House cottages were demolished and in 1831 two new rooms were added to the Workhouse.

The New Poor Law of 1834 aimed to cut costs by the more efficient organisation of relief and to reduce the demand for relief by making the conditions under which it was provided so harsh that only the truly desperate would seek it. Small parish workhouses were to be replaced by large Union Workhouses. The Ewell Workhouse was closed and sold off, the proceeds going towards a new Union Workhouse in Dorking Road, Epsom, close to where the hospital is now.

Relief to the poor was restricted to those considered to have a legal right to it, as laid down by the various Acts, and in particular the Act of Settlement of 1662, which gave powers to the Overseers of the Poor, on complaint to a Justice of the Peace, to return to their parish of settlement any newcomers to the parish who had no legal settlement within it. A person's Parish of Settlement was that in which he or she was born, in the absence of proof of entitlement on other grounds. A married woman could take her husband's parish as her own. A legitimate child took its father's Settlement, but a child born out of wedlock was deemed to be settled in the parish of its birth, even if the mother was not in residence there. A bastard child would not be accepted by the mother's parish if it was likely to become a charge on the rates, and could be forcibly separated from its mother and remain so for the rest of its life. A pregnant woman likely to have a child that would become a charge on the Poor Rates would be carted off to her Parish of Settlement.

The Act of Settlement was zealously applied to keep down the cost of relief by making sure that it was not granted to any pauper that could be forced onto some other parish. If there was any doubt, the pauper was examined by Justices of the Peace who gave a ruling on its Parish of Settlement. The parish identified would often appeal and there would then be a court case at the Quarter Sessions. Records of some of the cases dealt with are available in the Ewell Parish Examinations and Bastardy Papers from which the following are typical examples:

> To the Churchwardens and Overseers of the Poor of Ewell and of Charlwood. Whereas Complaint has been made by you, the Churchwardens and Overseers of the Poor of Ewell, unto us two of His Majesty's J.Ps that Mary —, single woman, hath lately intruded into Ewell there to inhabit contrary to the Laws relating to the Settlement of the Poor and is likely to be chargeable if not timely prevented. Upon examination and enquiry upon Oath of the said Mary — it appears that Mary — is like to become chargeable to Ewell and that the last legal Place of Settlement of Mary — is in Charlwood. To be conveyed from Ewell to Charlwood. 2nd August, 1762 Thomas Howard, Edward Northey.

There is an entry in the Ewell Overseers Account Book: Carrying Mary —— to Charlwood £1 1s. 10d.

> To the Constable of the Parish of Ewell and to all other Constables in the County of Surrey. Whereas Sarah —, single woman, hath by her voluntary examination taken in writing upon oath before me, Sir George Glyn, Bt., one of His Majesty's J.Ps, this present day declared herself to be with child and that the said child is likely to be born a bastard and to be chargeable to the Parish of Ewell, and that Henry — of Beddington did beget the said child on the body of her that said Sarah —. And whereas John Allingham, one of the Overseers of the Poor of Ewell, hath applied to me to issue my warrant for the apprehending of the said Henry —. To apprehend Henry — and bring him before a J.P to find security to indemnify the Parish of Ewell or else find sufficient surety for his appearance at the next Quarter Sessions.
> Given under my hand and Seal the Twenty Ninth Day of July, 1783 Geo. Glyn.

Elizabeth — came to Ewell in the winter of 1777-8 with her illegitimate child, Sarah, aged about three years. Elizabeth was by now married, but this did not affect the status of Sarah. Someone complained to the Magistrates that the child had 'lately intruded into Ewell, there to inhabit as a Parishioner contrary to the laws relating to the Settlement of the Poor'. The Magistrates adjudged that Sarah's Parish of Settlement was the place of her birth, Putney, and ordered her removal from Ewell. The Overseers' Account Book includes an entry: 'To carrying the — child to Putney 8s.'

There is no further reference to little Sarah. Presumably she was sent to the Putney Workhouse and never saw her parents again.

On 7 April 1741 at the Quarter Sessions in Reigate, an appeal was made by the Church-wardens and Overseers of the Poor of the Parish of Armsworth, Middlesex, against an Order by Lord Baltimore and Joseph Shaw whereby Elizabeth a widow, and her children William aged about nine, Martha about seven, John about four and Hannah one, were removed from Ewell to Armsworth. After witnesses were heard the appeal was dismissed.

The Vestry minutes and the Overseers' Accounts provide information on how Ewell Parish gave help to the poor for which it took responsibility. This help was not confined to the inhabitants of the Workhouse: substantial Out Relief payments were made. In the second half of the 18th century regular weekly payments were being made to as many as 20 people, some of whom were needy adults and others child minders. Assistance was also given to meet special cases of need as they arose and this is best illustrated by a few extracts from the accounts.

> July 1760
> Cloathing Elizabeth — when she went to service, viz:
> Two Gowns, two pair of Hose, two Handkerchiefs, two Aprons, two Caps,
> a pair of Shoes and Buckles, a Hat and Ribbons £1 13s. 6d.
>
> October 1768
> Expenses on a man with a broken legg. 4s.
> Expenses to cloath Mary — 17s. 6d
>
> February 1780
> A Ring for Ann — 6s.
> Marrying Ann — with John — 15s.
> Their Wedding Dinner. 8s. 2d.
> Making the Wedding Suit. 2s. 10d.
>
> March 1781
> Mutton and wine for Edward — 9½d.
> Nursing of Edward — 1s. 6d.
> Necessaries for Edward — 9d.
> Nursing and sitting up with Edward — 6s.
> Coffin and shroud for Edward — 12s. 6d.
> Carrying Edward — to the ground. 5s.
> Beer for bearers. 1s. 4d.
> Burial dues 4s.

Much of the work of the Ewell Vestry was concerned with the appointment of officials to administer relief of the poor and the discussion of specific problems. The following brief extracts from the minutes of the Vestry meetings give a graphic account of how the poor were dealt with.

4 September 1805:
Wm. Broadbent the Overseer of Cuddington applied for leave for Ann —— to reside in the Workhouse of this Parish till after her lying in by giving a Proper Indemnification which was agreed to accordingly. It was also agreed to advertise William —— in one of the London Papers for Eloping from his wife and family and leaving them Chargeable to this Parish. Offering a Reward of five guineas for his Apprehension.

13 December 1816:
    The Committee report that they think it is advisable to enter into a Contract for the maintenance of the Poor for half a year rather than for a longer Period, inasmuch that there is reason to hope the price of flour and many other Articles may be cheaper at the expiration of that Time than they are at present. A Contract so made if not more advantageous will at least be reduced to a greater certainty. The Committee are of the opinion it is necessary to reduce the Quality of the flour at least Ten Shillings per Sack and to regulate the present Bill of Fare.

27 June 1833:
    At the Quarterly Vestry held this day - It was unanimously Resolved that the Overseers be empowered to expend any Sum not exceeding Thirty pounds for the purpose of sending Mrs —— and her two children to her husband at Van Dieman's Land.

9 September 1833:
    It was Resolved that the Overseers do immediately procure a warrant for the apprehension of James —— for having deserted his wife and family who are now in the Poor House.

6 February 1834:
    It was Resolved that the Widows should have the privilege (for the present year) of getting their gowns made by whom they thought proper on condition that they do appear at the Church on Sunday morning, March 9th, in their new Clothing after Morning Service.

25 May 1854:
    It was recommended by the Vestry that the Board of Guardians be requested to allow not less than Ten Pounds for Widow —— to emigrate to Australia.

10 April 1863:
    It having come to the knowledge of this Vestry that the Tradesmen have supplied goods to the Poor before the issue of the tickets. Resolved that this custom is hereby condemned and that notice be given to the several Tradesmen that they will forfeit the right of supplying goods to the poor for the ensuing year by such an act.

It is clear from some of the extracts quoted that the implementation of the Poor Laws involved much harsh treatment of the poor, particularly those not considered to be the responsibility of the parish. Kindness and humanity were not entirely lacking, however, and given the difficult social conditions of the 18th and 19th centuries it seems likely that the poor of Ewell fared better than in many other parishes. It is significant that after the Workhouse proper was set up in 1781 relief was still being provided for people not living in the Workhouse. In some parishes it was a matter of 'Go into the Workhouse or go without'.

49. The Union Workhouse in Epsom was built following the New Poor Law of 1834, and took the poor previously housed in the Ewell Workhouse in West Street.

Enclosures

The Register gives a picture of Ewell in 1408 and similarly the Thomas Taylor Survey sets the scene for 1577. There is another date of similar significance, 1803, the year of the enclosure awards for Ewell, of which extensive records are available. The open field, strip system of cultivation that had been practised since Saxon times was extremely inefficient and a waste of time and labour because each man's strips were widely scattered. The use of common land was not conducive to rearing good cattle, since it provided no shelter and the mingling of cattle led to the spread of diseases among the herds. Land-owners began to see the advantages of re-organising the ownership and holding of land so that the strip system could be replaced by large homogeneous farms. This meant a general re-distribution of land, the dispossession of many small land-holders and the enclosure of commons. Such measures could only be taken when an Act of Parliament was passed and advocates of the scheme had to promote a bill for the enclosure of their particular village. Parliament usually passed the necessary act if the local lord the manor, the tithe owners and the owners of four-fifths of the strips were in favour.

50. Following the 1801 Act for enclosing Ewell, a detailed map of the parish was drawn up for the Commissioners to a scale of approximately 18 inches to a mile. This shows the centre of the village.

Enclosures started at least as early as the 16th century and often took the form of arable land and common land being enclosed for sheep, at times when there was a great demand for wool. There was however, a great increase in enclosures towards the end of the 18th century, reaching a peak between 1801 and 1810, and almost a quarter of all the land under cultivation was affected. A result of the Enclosure awards was that the class of peasant smallholders almost disappeared and agriculture became a three-tiered system of great land-owners, tenant farmers and landless labourers.

The Bill for enclosing Ewell was put forward in 1801 and the awards were made in 1803. The main promoters of the Bill were the Lord of the Manor, William Northey, the rector, Sir George Glyn, the 2nd Baronet who died in 1814, and Thomas Calverley, who owned the three sub-manors as well as other property. The opening wording was 'An Act for dividing and inclosing the common fields, common meadows, commons and waste lands within the Parish of Ewell in the County of Surrey. Whereas there are within the Parish of Ewell several common fields, common meadows, commons and waste lands, containing together by estimation one thousand, two hundred acres or thereabouts, which said common fields lie intermixed and dispersed, and with the said commons and waste lands in their present state incapable of any considerable improvement'. It then went on to ask that the land in question 'should be divided and inclosed and specific allotments made to the several parties according to their respective rights and interests, which would tend greatly to the improvements of their several estates'.

A detailed plan of Ewell was drawn up for the Commissioners in 1802 showing the existing properties and the proposed allotments. It made reference to about 180 houses and cottages in the Parish. The plan was drawn to a scale of approximately 18 inches to a mile, and is the earliest large scale map of Ewell in existence. The Commissioners were expected to defray their expenses by selling off bits of common land and some 130 acres of common land were lost by this, from Ewell Marsh and Ewell Downs. Thomas Calverley bought 111 acres of Ewell Downs for £1,775. Some allotments were made to compensate individuals for loss of rights. William Northey, Lord of the Manor, was given 21 acres of Kingston Common, near Ruxley, in lieu of his manorial right to the soil. Sir George Glyn received nearly 300 acres in lieu of tithes, which included 188 acres of Ewell Common Field. Some 70 landholders, freehold or copyhold, are listed in the schedule, and apart from a few with very small holdings, all received allotments, mostly on the commons, but some on the common field, proportional to their original holdings. Thomas Calverley was allotted nearly 350 acres excluding the land he purchased from the Commissioners, while some allotments were less than half an acre. The Poor of Ewell were allotted just under one acre next to the workhouse.

The Act was a remarkably detailed bit of legislation as it not only listed all the land holdings in the parish of Ewell, but also made provision for the roads and footpaths over the common lands, and laid down how they were to be maintained. Even the rights to grass and herbage along the roads were carefully specified. Not a fraction of an acre of the parish was left unaccounted for.

Cloudesley Willis was rather bitter about the enclosures, particularly because no land was reserved for the public, not even a village green. As he remarked, 'the effect of the enclosures on the poor was that the peasant cultivators disappeared and became labourers. Under the old system a poor man could obtain a small piece of land. After the enclosure the distress in Ewell was very great'. According to Margaret Glyn, however, in the introduction to the Register, 'Between 1577 and 1801 the tenants had ceased to cultivate, the furlongs were handed over to oblivion and the owners had so entirely neglected their rights that the Southfield lapsed into common down. The Commons Enclosure Act of 1801 gave the land into the hands of the leading residents in order that it might be cultivated, on account of the shortage of wheat caused by the war. The Surveys reveal that this cultivation was not in the case of Southfield a new departure but an agricultural renewal'.

Cloudesley Willis was not alone in feeling bitter about enclosures. Arthur Young, a writer of the period, quoted a popular verse that went:

Tis bad enough in man or woman to steal a goose from off a common
But surely he's without excuse who steals the common from the goose.

Chapter 9

The Glyn Family and the Church

I mentioned earlier how the advowson of the church passed through many hands after the dissolution of the monasteries. It would seem that the parish was not always well served with regard to the appointment of a parson. John Taylor, the self-styled Water-poet, commented in the early 17th century, 'It is most lamentable and remarkable that Ewell, a market town not much above 10 miles from London, in a Christian Kingdom hath neither Preacher nor pastor; for although the parsonage be able to maintain a sufficient preacher, yet the living being in a layman's hand is rented out to another for a great sum and yet no preacher is maintained there. The town is served with a poor old man that is half blind and by reason of his age can scarcely read. A sermon amongst them is as rare as warm weather in December, or ice in July: both of which I have seen in England, though but seldom'.[1]

Early in the 18th century the patronage was held by Sir Richard Bulkeley, who had a large estate in Ireland. According to Thomas Allen's *History of the Counties of Surrey and Sussex* : 'Sir Richard Bulkeley possessed considerable property and was a man of good sense and learning, but became entangled with a party of French enthusiasts who pretended to prophecy and so embarrassed his affairs that he was obliged to sell his estate. In his person he was very short and crooked and expected under the new dispensation to be made straight and handsome in a miraculous manner; but, to his great disappointment he died before the miracle was completed'.

Sir Richard died in 1710 aged 47 and was buried in the chancel of the old Ewell Church. In 1709 the estate had been acquired by Sir William Lewen who was Lord Mayor of London in 1717. His monument erected after his death in 1721 shows him in the appropriate finery. Sir William's great-niece, Susannah, who inherited the estate from her father, married Richard Glyn, who became the first of the Ewell Glyn baronets.[2] Their son, George, 1739-1814, became the second baronet,[3] and his elder son, Lewen Powell Glyn, became the third baronet. When Lewen Powell Glyn died in 1840 his brother the Revd. George Lewen Glyn became the fourth baronet. The Revd. George Glyn was born in 1804 and in 1831 was appointed vicar by his brother. When he became the fourth baronet in 1840 he was both patron of the living and vicar, and dominated Ewell for more than 40 years. His diaries give a vivid account of his efforts to bring the light to Ewell.

29 June 1842 – Mr X, a farmer, told me he approved of the best way but loved the worst and could not overcome temptations. I pointed out to him the love of God and the suffering of Jesus, that he might be led by the Spirit. This man came to the Sacraments Tuesday last. I have seen him drunk in his own home since. He died one day suddenly.

4 August 1843 – Mrs Cox, a market gardener's wife, told me in reply to a remonstrance on the employment of a Sunday School boy in driving birds from the fruit trees, that the birds would eat on a Sunday as well as weekdays, but she added, she did not know which ate the most, the birds or the boy. I replied - no marvel. If a boy's Sunday is so spent, where is he to get the principle to resist temptation ?

48

August 1859 – I commenced this month to visit the Parish poor again from house to house, for several years I had left this to my Curate and only visited the Upper and Middles Classes and one or two cases of the sick poor occasionally when there happened to be only a very few of the other classes sick. I feel this to have been a great mistake and am thankful to the Lord for several sharp hits from enemies as well as kind hints from friends which have induced me to amend the error. I have already visited two districts and begun a third this month so that I feel I can easily get through the Parish in a few months if spared. My renewed labor has been amply rewarded, I feel that if I could only compass the poor in the Parish once a year it will give me a vantage ground which naught else can supply.

The Rev. George Glyn (later Sir George) had his father's Queen-Anne house replaced by a new house built by Henry Duesbury in 1839. It is now called Glyn House and is owned by the Surrey County Council and used for educational purposes. Sir George found the old church in need of repair and proposed that it should be rebuilt on a new site which he offered to donate provided that a village right-of-way that passed too close to the windows of his new rectory could be moved. There was considerable opposition to destroying the old church but Sir George had his way and the work went ahead. It was agreed to leave the tower standing and make it into a mortuary chapel, but it is no longer in use. The tower was scheduled as an ancient monument in 1951 and a trust has been set up for its preservation. A wrought iron gate made by the local blacksmith, Mr. Ralph, has been fitted as a memorial to Cloudesley Willis, who died in 1955 at the age of ninety.

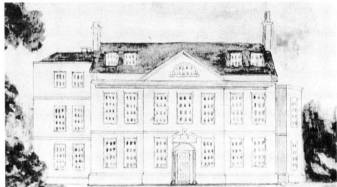

51. The Queen-Anne house, seen here in an 1825 water-colour, was demolished when Sir George Lewen Glyn had the Rectory, now known as Glyn House, built in 1839.

The new church was designed by Henry Clutton of Hartswood, near Reigate. He died in 1895 and is buried nearby in the churchyard at Sidlow Bridge church, which he also designed.[4]

The foundation stone of the new St Mary's was laid in June 1847 and was followed by the consecration service in August 1848. It was a remarkably quick building operation: no wonder Cloudesley Willis reported that his aunts' dresses stuck to the freshly varnished pews during the service. A Surrey newspaper gave a report on the consecration service, which was conducted by the Bishop of Winchester. It was stated that 'the old church was in a hopeless state of decay and the churchyard so full that the soil was raised nearly five feet above its original level. One large pew in the new building was set aside for the aged poor. A marquee was erected on the lawn, near the residence of Sir G. Glyn in which an elegant cold collation was spread, to which the clergy and their ladies were invited. The children of the schools were afterwards regaled with tea. The day was quite a holiday. A large flag was hoisted in the village, and there could not have been less than fifteen hundred people present, among whom were the greater part of the neighbouring gentry.'

52. The Lewen memorial shows Sir William, dressed in Lord Mayor of London regalia, and was brought from the old church. He died in 1721.

53. The nave and chancel of St Mary's church . The 15th-century chancel screen came from the old church.

54. St. Mary's church was built in 1847-8 by Henry Clutton in Gothic Revival style. Furnishings and memorials were transferred from the old church which was then demolished, although the tower was left standing.

55. Some attractive wall plaques were put up in the entrance hall of the rectory after the addition was made towards the end of the last century.

56. The rectory built by Henry Duesbury is shown in this photograph of a 1867 water colour painting.

57. Glyn House in 1992. The section on the right with the bay was added towards the end of the last century, while that on the left is a more recent addition.

58. The pulpit of St Mary's was donated by E. W. Martin in 1897 and is of marble and alabaster.

59. The Rev. George Lewen Glyn was appointed vicar in 1831 and became the fourth baronet in 1840. He dominated Ewell for more than 40 years.

St Mary's church consists of a large nave with separately roofed aisles and chancel and a tower at the north-west corner. The west window is a memorial to Emma Gadesden, who lived in Ewell Castle for many years; the portraits in the medallions at the top are possibly of Emma herself. The bells and clock were transferred from the old church, as well as various other fittings, including the altar, the rood screen and the 15th-century font. In 1897 the Tudor oak pulpit was replaced by a pulpit of alabaster and marble donated by E. W. Martin of Nonsuch House. The reredos also dates from the end of the 19th century and was donated by Sir Gervas Glyn. The altar is a Jacobean wooden table made in 1612. The East window designed by James Hogan was installed in 1947, replacing one that was damaged during air raids. The small north window is even more recent having been put in following damage to the north aisle by fire in 1973.

The Rev. Sir George Glyn married twice. His first wife died in 1854, leaving Sir George with a son and two daughters. Five years later he married his cousin once removed, Henrietta, who was 24 years his junior, and who had five children by him, three sons and two daughters. From letters and documents left behind by the Glyns a picture emerges of a comfortable well-to-do family life. The 1871 Census shows them as having two nurses, a cook, housemaid and parlourmaid living in and there were presumably a coachman, stable boy and gardeners living elsewhere. When Sir George Glyn died in 1885 he was buried on the site of the altar of the old church. The tomb was renovated in 1985 on the centenary of his death.

GLYN
of Glynllivon
Carnarvonshire, and
Ewell Surrey

ΤΡΩΣΙΣ ΥΠΟ ΙΗΣΥΣ

60. When Sir George Glyn died in 1885 he was buried on the site of the altar of the old church. The tomb was renovated in 1985 on the centenary of his death.

On the death of Sir George his son by his first wife, George Turberville Glyn, became the 5th baronet. He died without heirs and Sir George's eldest son by his second wife, Gervas Powell Glyn, became the 6th baronet. He also died without heirs and as the second son had died in the army the youngest son, Arthur, became the 7th and last of the Ewell baronets. He never married and on his death the title passed to Sir Richard Fitzgerald Glyn of Dorset, 4th baronet Glyn of Gaunts, who then became 4th baronet Glyn of Gaunts and 8th baronet Glyn of Ewell.

Sir Arthur Glyn became the 7th baronet in 1921 and until his death in 1942 played a prominent part in local and county affairs, becoming a J.P. He lived in the Well House in Church Street, a pair of houses made into one and since separated again. The Rectory House, or Glyn House, as we now call it, became quite a social centre where big parties were laid on for the children of the village school in the music room, a separate large hall that Arthur and his sister Margaret had had built. In fact, Arthur Glyn took a great interest in the school and the annual Old Boys' Day which was a major event in the local calendar. There was also an old boys' cricket team that he supported. The two daughters of Sir George, Anna and Margaret, deserve a few words. Anna was a talented writer and had two novels published. In 1895 she had some teeth extracted under chloroform at her home and died a month later at the age of 35: it was a sad end for a lively girl who left behind a spirited account of adventurous travels in the Middle East, in Australia and Ceylon. Margaret was a composer and musicologist who wrote articles on early English composers and with her brother Gervas collected old musical

61. Anna Glyn, the sister of Margaret, was a talented writer and had two novels published. She gave a lively account of travels in the Middle East, Australia and Ceylon. She died at the age of 35.

62. Margaret was a daughter of the Rev. Sir George Glyn by his second wife, Henrietta, 24 years his junior. She was a composer and musicologist, and with her brother Gervas collected old musical instruments.

63 & 64. Arthur Glyn, a brother of Margaret and Anne, became the 7th baronet in 1921. He played a prominent part in local and county affairs, becoming a J.P.

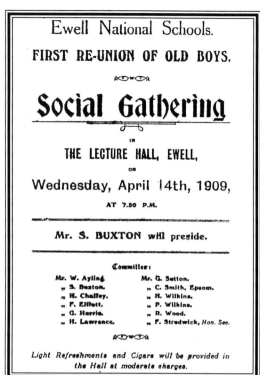

65. Henrietta Amelia Glyn, second wife of Sir George Lewen Glyn, the daughter of Richard Carr Glyn, photographed by Monsieur A. Boucher of 23 Ship Street, Brighton 'just below the Post Office'.

66 & 67. A notice advertising the first reunion of the Ewell Old Boys in 1909, and the programme of events.

PROGRAMME.

ᴖ PART I. ᴖ

Part Songs	"Old Lang Syne" "Old King Cole" "Harmony"	Present Scholars
Song	"Boys Together"	Mr. W. Ayling
Song	"Mona"	Mr. R. Mason, jun.
Song	"Out in the Bay"	Mr. A. H. Spikesman
Comic Song	"Jolly Well Serves You Right"	Mr. Roger Ayling
Recitation	"A Woman's Curiosity"	Mr. J. Davey
Glee	"Spring's Delights"	Old Boys
Song	"The King's Own"	Mr. A. Gordon
Song	"The Song that will Live for Ever"	Mr. T. Westing
Song	"As your Hair Grows Whiter"	Mr. J. Charman
Recitation	"On Strike"	Mr. H. Wilkins
Duet	"Excelsior"	Mr. W. Ayling „ G. Harris
Song	"Thora"	Mr. W. H. Sparrow

Address by W. MELMOTH WALTERS, Esq.

INTERVAL.

ᴖ PART II. ᴖ

Glees	"The Three Chafers" "O! Who will o'er the Downs"	Old Boys
Song	"The Powder Monkey"	Mr. A. Gordon
Song	"Homeland, Good-bye"	Mr. W. Westing
Song	"Out on the Deep"	Mr. F. Strudwick
Comic Song	"When Father put his New Suit on"	Mr. Roger Ayling
Recitation	"The Man before the Mast"	Mr. W. Herbert
Concertina Solo	Selections	Mr. J. Ayling
Song	"On the Banks of Bonnie Loch Lomond"	Mr. W. Burden
Song	"I Don't Care if There's a Girl There"	Mr. H. Wilkins
Song	"My Old Shako"	Mr. W. H. Sparrow
Song	"Annie Laurie"	Mr. R. Mason, jun.
Song	"Love Me, and the World is Mine"	Mr. H. Ayling
Song	"Sons of the Sea"	Mr. W. Ayling

"GOD SAVE THE KING."

68. The Old Boys of Ewell National Schools had an annual reunion that started in 1909. This was taken shortly after that date. They later became the Old Boys' Association.

69. The Ewell Old Boys procession led by a band, *c*.1911.

70. The Old Boys were entertained at the Rectory, and were clearly a well-balanced crowd.

71. Arthur Glyn also supported the Ewell Old Boys' cricket team who are seen here, *c*.1912.

instruments which were housed in the converted Malt House in Church Street which is now the church of St Michael, Brotherhood of Universal Truth. After her death in 1946 the collection was dispersed. Margaret Glyn was an active member of the National Trust and gave land to them including Hatch Furlong to be part of the green belt. In 1925 she bought Bourne Hall to keep it out of the hands of the developers, and later sold it to the borough council in the hope that it would be preserved. With regard to the use of the rectory referred to, it is of interest that Glyn House today is occasionally the venue for local social events.

Until it was pulled down in 1905, the timber Rectory Farmhouse stood between the church and the old church tower. At one time the uncle of the artist Holman Hunt lived there, and this was one of the reasons for Pre-Raphaelite artists being associated with Ewell.[5]

72. The memorial to James Lowe, the inventor of a screw propeller, was designed by his daughter Henrietta. He was run over and killed by a waggon in Blackfriars Road in 1866.

Mention has been made of the tomb of Sir George Glyn in the churchyard of St Mary's. There are many other interesting graves to be seen there, including that of an inventor, James Lowe, whose epitaph reads: 'Sacred to the memory of James Lowe, Esquire, who was born May 18th, 1798 and met his death from an accident the 12th October, 1866. He was the inventor of the segments of the screw propeller, in use since 1838; and his life, though unobtrusive, was not without great benefit to his country. He suffered many troubles but bore them lightly as his hope was not in this world, but in his Saviour'.

James Lowe was a Scot and he married the eldest daughter of 'Squire' Barnes of Ewell. She brought him £3,000, most of which he spent on experiments to make a successful screw-driven ship. It is not claimed that he invented the screw propeller, but rather a special configuration of the blades which, together with a particular disposition of the propeller and shaft, gave the ship a good turn of speed. He became involved in law suits to defend his invention and although he was successful the cost ruined him. In 1866 he was run over by a waggon in Blackfriars Road. James Lowe's work was carried on by his daughter, Henrietta, who married a Frederick Vansittart. In 1868 Henrietta took out a patent for a propeller known as the Lowe-Vansittart propeller, and was able to persuade the Admiralty to try it out on a corvette. It performed well but for some

73. Rectory Farm, where the artist Holman Hunt visited his uncle William Hobman, stood close to the tower of the old church. It was demolished in 1905, shortly after this photograph was taken.

obscure reason they did not take it up. All in all, she was a remarkable person: there were not many lady engineers around in those days. She even designed her father's memorial, and presumably forgave him for spending what should have been her inheritance with so little return.

Not all the inhabitants of Ewell toed the party line in their religion: it is on record that in 1669 there were 50 Nonconformists. A report of 1725 refers to Ewell having about 50 Presbyterians. Nonconformists were also active in the 19th century. A remarkable domestic servant, Mary Wallis, who started work at the age of nine for a Mr G. B. Stone in Ewell, saved enough of her meagre wages to have a small wooden chapel built in West Street in the face of a considerable lack of sympathy from the local establishment. It opened in 1825 and preachers were found to give regular services. After eight years Mary lost control of the chapel, and in 1845 the lease was surrendered to Sir George Glyn, who was granted a new lease and had the chapel licensed for Episcopal worship. It would have been found very useful during the period in which the new parish church was being built and the old one demolished, after which the chapel ceased to be used for worship and became a carpenter's shop.

74. Mary Wallis was a domestic servant who saved enough of her meagre wages to have a small wooden chapel built in West Street where services were held for a number of years. Later, she was a founder member of the Congregational Church and died at the age of 90 in 1879.

75. The small wooden chapel that Mary Wallis had built in West Street in 1825 was restored and reopened by the Congregational Church as the Mary Wallis Hall in 1930. In the restoration, timbers were used from two obsolete wooden battleships, H.M.S. *Duncan* and H.M.S. *Impregnable*.

76. All Saints' church was enlarged in the early 1970s by the addition of the south aisle.

77. John Henry Bridges of Ewell Court, a descendant of the gunpowder manufacturers, established a fund and donated a plot of land on the Ewell Court Estate on which All Saints' church was built in 1893-4 as a daughter church of St Mary's. West Ewell became an independent parish in 1952.

78. The Ewell Congregational Church was built in 1864-5 in the High Street (or Greenman Street, as that particular stretch of road was then called) on a triangular plot of land now maintained as the Longhurst Memorial Garden. This architect's drawing was used when an appeal for contributions towards the cost of the building was made to the Christian Public in 1864.

In 1865 a Congregational church was founded in a new, more substantial chapel built in what is now the High Street, largely through the efforts of Mr. John Carr Sharpe, one of the owners of the gunpowder mills. Mary Wallis was one of the church's founder members. She died in 1879 aged 90. The church in the High Street was eventually found to be inadequate, and a new church, now a United Reformed church, was opened in 1938 in London Road. The little chapel that Mary Wallis had built was not forgotten; in 1908 it came on the market and was bought by two members of the Congregational Church, and was later acquired by the church, renovated and opened as the Mary Wallis Hall in 1930. It remained in use until after the new church was built in 1938 and was demolished soon after. A new Mary Wallis Memorial Hall was erected behind the church in 1939, but was destroyed by fire in 1966. It was not rebuilt in its original form; instead a room was dedicated to Mary Wallis in a subsequent extension to the church.

As will be mentioned later, in 1881 West Ewell was a self-contained community. It was a growing community and by the 1890s it needed its own church. John Henry Bridges of Ewell Court, a descendant of the gunpowder manufacturers, established a fund and donated a plot of land on the Ewell Court Estate on which All Saints church was built in 1893-4 as a daughter church of St Mary's. West Ewell became an independent parish in 1952. In 1975 a new community centre adjoining the church was opened.

Chapter 10

Ewell in 1881

The Census of 1881 and trade directories provide a snapshot of Ewell at the height of Victorian splendour: the Queen had been on the throne for more than 40 years and in 1877 had been proclaimed Empress of India. The long reign over Ewell of Sir George Lewen Glyn was coming to an end: he retired as vicar in 1881.

The population of the parish was 3,002, which included 559 pupils and staff of the Kensington and Chelsea Workhouse School in Fir Tree Road. This was a self-contained community and has been disregarded in our analysis. The population occupied 513 houses.

The local gentry residents included Mrs. Elizabeth Torr at Garbrand Hall, Mr. A. W. Gadesden at Ewell Castle, Sir George Glyn at the Rectory and also a retired general, a Major General, a barrister and a ship owner.

There was a wide range of shopkeepers and tradesmen which included four bootmakers, a bonnet maker, two drapers, two outfitters, five grocers, three butchers, four bakers as well as a general store, a fishmonger, three ironmongers (one of which was Henry Willis, the grandfather of Cloudesley Willis), a chemist, two builders, a blacksmith and a plumber. Other services were provided by a telegraphist, a fly driver, and a chimney sweep.

An interesting fact that emerges from the census information is that there was considerable mobility of workers. Out of a total of more than 700 men only 25 per cent had been born in Ewell. There were just over 200 women workers of whom 33 per cent had been born in the parish. Most of the 'immigrants' came from other parts of Surrey and south-east England, but a considerable number came from more far flung places, including Devon and Cornwall, Yorkshire, Wales, Ireland and Scotland. There was a cook born in Norway, a housemaid born in India and a labourer who was born at sea.

79. Mr. Marks' grocer's shop was in Kingston Road and is now a house called the Pedlars Rest.

80. Sir David Evans, 1849-1907, head of the firm of Richard Evans & Co., trimming manufacturers, Lord Mayor of London, 1891-2, lived at Ewell Grove. His recreations were hunting and shooting and he was Master of the West Surrey Staghounds, which met at Ewell Grove. He was the third Lord Mayor of London to be associated with Ewell.

81. Cracknell's butcher's shop around 1895. It stood close by the entrance to Bourne Hall and was demolished in the late 1980s.

Some of the upper- and middle-class residents also had a British India connection. Henrietta Glyn, wife of Sir George, and his sister in law Lydia were both born in India, as were two of the children of a retired Major General, whose wife had been born in Asia Minor and another daughter in Burma. The Headmaster of Grange School was born in India and a number of retired people also. These many associations with India in a place the size of Ewell are an indication of the ramifications of the Indian Adventure.

The place of birth of the wife of the Secretary of the British and Foreign Bible Society was given as Western Australia, while the one-year-old grand-daughter of Augustus Gadesden was born in Japan. Other residents had links with Italy, Spain, Germany and Switzerland.

Agriculture was still important: there were five large farms and several smaller ones. The chief crops were wheat, oats and barley. Nearly 120 men worked on farms, but domestic service now provided more jobs, 60 for men and more than 270 for women. It was inevitable that the varied social mix should give rise to class consciousness. A retired army officer is reported to have said that there was more caste in Ewell than in the whole of India.

The population included 794 children below 15 years of age. Only three men and

82. Strictly speaking, Mr. Robert Dearle should not appear, as his tallow chandler's shop was in Epsom, but how could one leave out a venerable old gentleman who witnessed 77 Derby races. This was taken in 1898.

eight women had reached the age of 80 and there was no-one over 90 years. Medical needs were met by two doctors. Refreshments were available from the Ewell Parochial rooms and there were also 13 public houses. There was a daily carrier service to London. Two fairs were held annually — one on 12 May for cattle and one on 29 October for sheep.[1]

The population growth pattern was:

1801 - 1112
1831 - 1630
1881 - 2443
1931 - 7117

It is difficult to give a comparable modern figure, because of boundary changes since 1931 but making an estimate based on the old boundaries gives a figure of about 19,000.

83. By the end of the last century there was a separate settlement at the end of West Street known as Gibraltar. Some of the mid-19th century weather-boarded cottages remain.

Ewell was described as a pleasant little town that was once a market town.[2] The 513 houses included a dozen or so sizeable residences, each employing at least six servants. The town was a separate entity, surrounded by fields, or rather several entities, since Gibraltar was a self-contained cluster of cottages at the end of West Street, and West Ewell was also separate. At the Dipping Place a spring of crystal water gushed forth. There was an abundance of timber framed buildings with numerous busy little shops shaded by fine trees and set in a street layout of subtle variety, altogether delightful.

It is clear that in 1881 Ewell was no longer a close-knit rural community largely dependent on agriculture. Its attractive situation around the springs and ready access from London had led to prosperous London merchants moving in and having large houses built. The process started in the 18th century, helped by the construction of the turnpike roads; the numerous Georgian houses in Spring Street and Church Street are its legacy. These large houses provided employment for many local people, as well as 'immigrants'. The coming of the railways in 1847 and 1859 accelerated the change to an economy dependent on wealth from outside.

Chapter 11

Industry and Transport

The Gunpowder Mills

Ewell has not been famous for its industries: however, there was one industry that sometimes became known outside the confines of Ewell. In 1812 an explosion at the gunpowder mills was heard as far away as Horsham. Gunpowder manufacture started at Ewell in the 18th century. Rocque's map of Surrey of 1762 showed the mills on the Hogsmill close to Ewell Court. They occupied a site of 45 acres, and at their peak employed 156 workers. For much of the time the Bridges family were the owners, but in 1862 the owners were Sharpe, Adams and Co. The change of ownership did not improve safety: in the early days there were explosions about every 20 years, but they became more frequent, an explosion in 1863 being followed by one in 1865 and two in 1871.[1] It is not surprising that in 1872 the Magistrates were asked by the Parish Vestry not to issue a licence to the company for the manufacture of cartridges. The mills closed in 1875, probably because the requirements of the Explosives Act of that year would have made them uneconomic. According to Cloudesley Willis, it was said in Ewell, at the time of the Franco-Prussian War, that the French were beaten because they used bad gun-powder manufactured at Ewell.

Sir George Glyn referred to the 1863 explosion in a diary entry of 20 April of that year: '... An awful catastrophe occurred last Wednesday morning at six a.m. Three men, James Baker, Henry Hockham and a single man, Weverman, only lately come had just started work in

84. The gunpowder mills, seen here at the end of the 19th century, were on the Hogsmill River north of Ewell. Manufacture started in the 18th century and continued until 1875. An explosion in 1812 was heard as far away as Horsham. The site has been thoroughly cleared.

85. James Baker was killed in an explosion at the gunpowder mills in 1863. There are other graves of victims of explosions in the churchyard.

86. Tombs of members of the Bridges family, owners of the gunpowder mills for many years.

the Corning House at the Powder Mill when it blew up, and instantaneously scattered their bodies in mangled pieces over the adjoining fields. ... On Sunday April 19 I held an open air service at the Powder Mills close to the spot where the accident happened and had an audience of eight or nine hundred. Mr. Sharpe, one of the owners, and his wife attended. He is a member of the Free Church of Scotland, and has seriously thought of opening a chapel here. He is opposed to the payment of Church Rates and is disposed to give trouble. It may be that this explosion may in God's hands prevent or at least delay his purpose.'

Victims of the explosions are buried in St Mary's churchyard, where there are also the tombs of members of the Bridges family, who owned the gunpowder mills for a considerable period and died in their beds.

The present Ewell Court was built on the site of Avenue House, at various times used by the mill owners and managers. The site of the gunpowder mills has been thoroughly cleared, and is now public land for recreation.

The Windmill

The Ewell Windmill, which stood just off Windmill Lane to the south of Ewell, was a smock mill built about 1750 and was in operation until 1883. It was demolished in about 1900. The mill house became a private residence and Tom Walls, the comedian and actor, lived there for many years. In a sale notice of 1853 the mill was described as 'A capital tower windmill with spring and cloth sails, driving three pairs of 4 ft French burr and one pair of Peak stones, with flour and smut machines' (the smut machine was for cleaning wheat).

87. Ewell Court, now a library, was built in 1879 on the site of Avenue House, at various times used by the mill owners and managers. It is near the site of Worth Court, the manor house of the principal manor of Ewell.

88. Ewell Windmill was a smock mill and stood to the south of Ewell village from about 1750 until about 1900. This shows it in 1801.

Bricks, tiles and pottery

The Jehovah's Witnesses' meeting place in London Road is a reminder of the brick, tile and pottery making that went on in the last century in that area. The building opened as *The Brick Burners beer house* in 1851 but by 1871 the name had been changed to *The Brick Kiln*. It ceased to be a pub and was taken over by the Jehovah's Witnesses in 1955. The pub supplied beer to the workers in one gallon jars. The products of the Nonsuch Works included bricks, tiles, chimney pots, flower pots and bread bins. Some of the chimney pots were particularly fine specimens.

89. The Kingdom Hall before 1955 was the *Brick Kiln* public house. A beer house named the *Brick Burners* had opened there in about 1851. Beer was supplied to the workers of the brick and tile works across the road in 'khaki babies' (one gallon stone jars).

Transport

After the Romans left England their roads were neglected and long stretches were no longer used. However, the modern road from London Bridge to Ewell is largely on the route of Stane Street and it is likely that it has been in more or less continuous use since Roman times. In medieval times it was known as the Kings Highway to London. But apart from that, roads capable of taking wheeled vehicles were more or less non-existent and communication and trade were by means of bridle paths and pack horses.

Increasing trade throughout the country led to demands for better roads, and from the end of the 17th-century Turnpike Trusts were authorised by Parliament to construct roads. An Act of 1737 which was an extension of an earlier act included provision for a road 'between Nonsuch and Worcester Parks in Cuddington near Ewell', which is the present London Road. The road from Ewell to Cheam was authorised by an Act of 1755, which also included the construction of roads from Tooting to Ewell (the A24) and from Ewell across the common fields to Burgh Heath (the present Reigate Road) and from Epsom through Ewell to Kingston.[2] The old Reigate Road still exists as a small road that crosses the Priesthill Playing Fields, once part of the Southfield.

The improved roads brought coaches. Before 1834 when the link from London Road to the High Street was constructed, the coaches went along Church Street and stopped at the *King's Head*, a hostelry acquired by Sir George Glyn in 1850 and converted to housing. A reminder of the coach traffic along Church Street is the grave of 22-year-old Catherine Bailey in St Mary's churchyard. She was killed in 1826 when the Dorking coach overturned in the High Street, the horses having been started accidentally when the coach had been standing outside the *King's Head*. The *Spring Hotel* also was much used by coaches.

90. The bridge over a branch of the Hogsmill River near Ewell Court is known as the Packhorse Bridge and is thought to be 18th-century, restored at various periods. This view shows it shortly before the Second World War.

91. The Horse Pond was not used only by horses. A travelling circus made use of it early this century.

92. The Horse Pond in the early days of this century, when it really was used by horses.

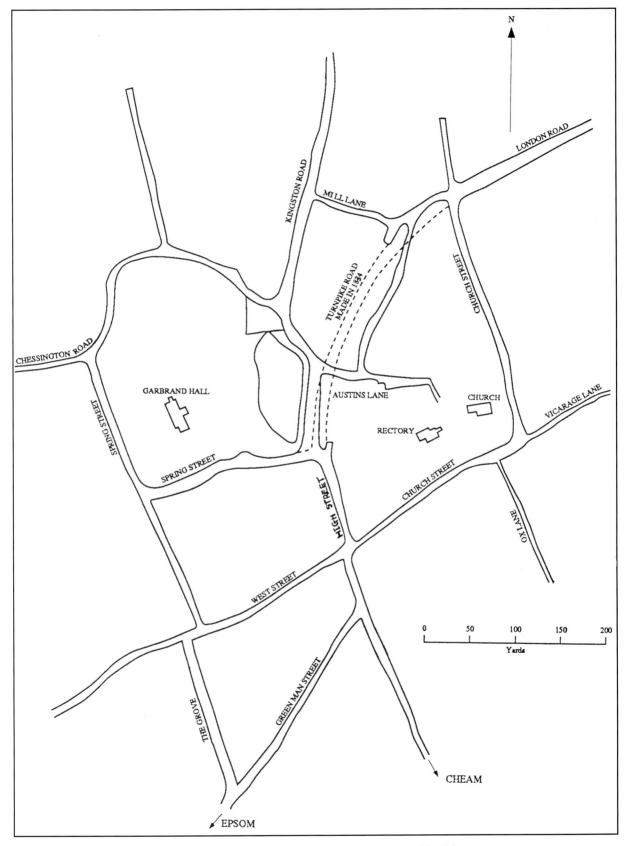

93. Ewell, before the turnpike road was constructed in 1834.

94. The railway engine *Ewell* built in 1875 was one of a series known as the Brighton Terriers, designed by William Stroudley for the London, Brighton and South Coast Railway.

95. The Stroudley Brighton Terrier *Waddon* was built in 1875. After service in various capacities, it was shipped to Montreal for inclusion in the Canadian Railroad Transport Museum in 1963.

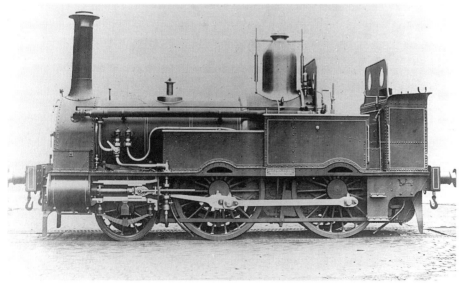

96. A London and South Western Railway locomotive made to Beattie's patent in 1875.

97. Ewell West Station, shown early this century, was originally the Ewell station of the London & South Western Railway and opened in 1859.

98. The *Railway Hotel* near Ewell East Station, then the Ewell station of the London, Brighton and South Coast Railway, was built in 1854. This shows it towards the beginning of this century, by which time it was known as the *Glyn Arms*.

Ewell was on the London to Leatherhead via Epsom coach route. After Leatherhead the coaches went to such destinations as Dorking, Horsham, Littlehampton, Worthing, Bognor and Guildford. The coach time from London (*The Bull*, Holborn) to Epsom was 2½ hours. A typical coach would be licensed to seat four people inside and eleven on the top, and would be drawn by four horses. In 1836, the peak time for coaches, as the competition from the railways soon increased, there were at least nine coaches a day through Ewell coming from London, and of course the same number in the opposite direction. In the days when they all used Church Street there must have been the occasional traffic jam.

The railways came to Ewell in 1847, when the station now known as Ewell East was opened on 10 May. It was on the Croydon to Epsom via Sutton section of the London, Brighton and South Coast Railway, a section which was to have been operated as an atmospheric railway. This was a system on which the train had no locomotive; instead it was propelled by a piston travelling in a continuous iron tube 15 inches in diameter laid between the tracks. The piston was sucked along the tube by exhausting the air by means of stationary engines installed in pumping houses situated at intervals along the track. The system had been operated, apparently successfully, on several lines, including one from Croydon to Forest Hill, on which a speed of 44½ miles an hour was claimed. However, the design imposed severe restrictions on track layout. Furthermore, it involved a slot along the top of the tube sealed by a strip of leather that was lifted as the connecting rod travelled along, a valve mechanism that was ingenious but not sufficiently reliable for hard use in the heat of the summer and cold of the winter. Regardless of the many thousands of pounds that had been spent on it the atmospheric railway went out of favour and the Croydon to Epsom line was completed as a conventional steam railway. An 1887 timetable shows journey times from Ewell to London Bridge via West Croydon ranging from 46 to 61 minutes.

The Ewell station of the London and South Western Railway, now known as Ewell West, opened when the line from Raynes Park to Epsom was commissioned on 4 April 1859. An 1860 timetable shows eight trains a day from Ewell to Waterloo with journey times ranging from 27 to 35 minutes. However, it bears a note: 'While this line is in bad order an extra five minutes to be taken on each journey'. The London, Brighton and South Coast Railway and the London and South Western Railway went their own ways until merged by the Railways Act of 1921.[3] The line through Ewell West was electrified in 1925 and through Ewell East in 1929.

As may be imagined, the standard of comfort on the early railways left much to be desired, particularly for third class passengers. Open carriages were common until a law in 1854 insisted on closed vehicles with windows. There was no heating, although first class passengers were supplied with small foot warmers containing hot water at 6d. a time. The railways did as much as anything to transform Ewell into a dormitory town.

99. The mid-19th-century *Star* in Cheam Road ceased to be a public house in the 1960s and part was incorporated with the adjoining timber-framed building at the junction with the High Street.

100. The High Street, *c*.1900, from the junction with Cheam Road, looking north.

101. This building in Church Street was the *King's Head Inn* in the days when the street was used by coaches. It dates mainly from the early 19th century.

102. A photograph of the High Street in about 1890, looking towards the junction with Church Street.

103. The High Street, looking north, in the 1920s.

104. Greenman Street, now High Street, *c.*1900, looking north towards the junction with Cheam Road. The spire of the Congregational Chapel pulled down shortly after 1938 can be seen, and the signboard of the *Lord Nelson* demolished in 1963.

105. The High Street in 1992 looking towards the site of the Congregational Chapel.

Chapter 12

Schools

National Schools were founded by the Church of England National Society for the Education of the Poor in 1811 and Ewell School was founded in 1816 in a couple of cottages in Old Schools Lane which were demolished in 1964.

From the beginning two local charities, Brumfields and Whites, made contributions to the school and it benefited in 1860 with £200 received in consequence of the will of Thomas Calverley. From 1854, 20 poor children were nominated yearly by the Vestry to receive free education, from eight to eleven years of age, ten boys and ten girls. The parents of other children were expected to pay on a graduated scale, depending on their employment. A new National School was opened in West Street in 1861 and was in use until the new school was opened in 1971. The old school still stands in West Street although it is no longer used as a school.

106. West Street in about 1920, close to the National school built in 1861.

When the Education Act of 1870 made elementary education available to all children, existing Church Schools carried on as before but assisted by government grants. Parents were still charged a small weekly fee, unless they were very poor. Before the advent of free schools in 1891, the charge for the child of a tradesman or small farmer in Ewell was 6d., for the first child of a labourer it was 2d. and a penny for each additional child.

It was reported by an elderly resident that at the beginning of this century the school was divided into three sections. The ground floor front was for boys aged between seven and fourteen years of age. The first floor, reached by a stone outside staircase at the rear of the building, was for girls aged seven to fourteen and the ground floor rear was for mixed infants of five to seven years old. The principal accommodation was large halls divided into three classes by curtains. In 1913 a new school building farther down West Street was opened for girls and infants, so that the boys had the old building to themselves.

According to the Vestry Minutes, there was a Bonnet and Cloak Fund from 1843 to 1854, which, 'Sir John and Lady Rae Reid having kindly presented the Ewell National School with sixty bonnets, the object of this fund is to keep up and repair the bonnets, cloaks, aprons and capes worn by the girls of the school at church'.

In 1862 head teachers were instructed to keep daily records in a log book, with an injunction that an entry once made must not be altered. Inspectors reported on the school and staff. The log book of the Ewell National Boys' School from 1862 to 1898 has survived and enables a picture of the life of the school to be built up. According to the inspector's report of January 1863, 'the character of the school may on the whole be pronounced a fair one, particularly as regards the Master's intentions'. A reminder that Ewell was a rural area is that the August holiday was known as the harvest holidays and in 1871 it was extended for a week 'as gleaning was not over'.

107. When this school was erected in West Street in 1913 it took girls and infants, so that the West Street boys then had the 1861 building to themselves.

108. Ewell class four boys, 1907. The Ewell Boys school, E.B.S., was popularly known as eggs, bacon and sausages.

109. The Ewell Boys school was proud of its football team.

110. The school, shown here in 1992, was opened in West Street in 1861, and initially housed all the school children.

111. West Street School mixed infants class, 1897. Until 1913, when the new building was put up, the boys, girls and infants shared the 1861 school.

112. Ewell Infants class 3, 1907.

113. The 'big girls' of the West Street school, early this century.

As might be expected, the epidemics prevalent in the second half of the last century are reflected in the log book. The school had to be closed for three weeks in 1874 because of an outbreak of measles in which two boys died. In 1879 scarlet fever caused closure for ten weeks. Diphtheria, mumps, whooping cough and smallpox also figure in the entries. Measles, scarlet fever and whooping cough came to the village almost every year.

Boys will be boys and an entry for 17 December 1872 reads, 'two boys, the sweepers, had burnt holes in the floor and the Master's table with a red hot poker and that the Monitor was also playing in the classroom after school with tongs that he had made red hot. Also found the two sweepers had deliberately and wilfully broken off two of the hat pegs last Friday evening on going out of school. These two boys were punished with the cane'.

Life at the school was not all disease and violence. On 22 September 1883 a half-day holiday was given so that the boys could go to the circus in Epsom. There were outings such as one to London on 23 July 1894, which took in the Houses of Parliament, Westminster Abbey, Government Offices, the Monument, the Tower, Tower Bridge, St Paul's, Trafalgar Square and the Zoo. The boys had saved up for it by weekly subscriptions. The observance of old country customs also provided diversions. There are references to 'maying' on 1 May, Garland Day, and the annual kicking of a football made from the bladder of a horse through the streets of the village on Shrove Tuesday.

In 1870 the number of boys on the register was 60 but by 1897 it was 135, an increase that could be accounted for by the Compulsory Education Act as well as the growing population. In 1898, the end of the period covered by the log book, the school staff consisted of the Master, an Assistant Master, a Pupil Teacher and two Monitors.

Chapter 13

Ewell Parochial Charities

The ancient parish of Ewell no longer exists; as the population has grown, new churches have been built, new parishes carved out of the old ecclesiastical parish, and the civil parish is now part of the borough of Epsom and Ewell. However, the ancient parish still exists in the eyes of the Charity Commissioners because old charities are still in existence. The bequests were for the benefit of the needy within the parish at the time, and are still administered in that way. Since Kingswood was administered by the Ewell Parish Vestry prior to its constitution as a new parish with a portion of Banstead in 1838, Kingswood residents are eligible to benefit from Ewell parochial charities established prior to that date. The worthy benefactors of the various charities deserve to be remembered.

Henry Smith

Henry Smith was born in Wandsworth in about 1548. He is reputed to have been a silversmith, and he was an Alderman of the City of London. Records that would have given more information about him were destroyed in the Great Fire of London. Henry Smith went into the property market in a big way, and when he died in 1627 was in possession of extensive estates, which included the manors of Knole, Sevenoaks and Seele in Kent, Warbleton, Southwicke and Eastbrook in Sussex. He also owned land in Kensington, Chelsea and Westminster. Smith endowed a large number of charities in Surrey and appointed trustees to administer them. The towns of Croydon, Kingston, Guildford, Farnham, Godalming and Dorking were each given £1,000 for the relief and maintenance of the poor and smaller bequests were allotted to every parish in Surrey, mainly in the form of rents from land which were to be distributed by the churchwardens and the Overseers of the Poor.

According to the conditions laid down, 'They should distribute the said rents for the relief of aged poor or infirm people, married persons having more children born in lawful wedlock than their labours could maintain, poor orphans, such poor people as should keep themselves and families to labour and should put forth their children apprentices at the age of 15, and not to or for the relief of any persons who are given to excessive drinking, whoremongers, common swearers, pilferers, or otherwise notoriously scandalous, or to any persons that have been incorrigible or disobedient to those whose servants they have been, or to any vagrants, or such as should not have inhabited in the parish for five years next before the distribution or being able should refuse to work'.

The allocation to Ewell was 1/16th part of the annual income of an estate at Worth in Sussex. The original allocation to Ewell amounted to £10 a year. The amount received for the year ending Michaelmas 1989 was £3,000. In 1845, implementation of the Poor Laws led the Ewell Vestry Clerk to query the distribution of the charity with the Trustees. The Trustees replied, 'We did not understand the inquiry made by your Vestry Clerk or we should have discussed it more fully. Mr. Smith's gift is to the Poor of the Parish and he expressed a wish that those who have lived five years in the parish should be the objects selected. We consider it perfectly immaterial whether they have a legal settlement or legal claim to relief. As the laws for the relief of the Poor could not have been contemplated by Mr. Smith nor could they deprive any poor person of the benefit he intended for them. Every Parish in Surrey has some portion of the gift'.

Thomas Dickinson

Thomas Dickinson, a skinner, directed in his will of 1631 that all the residue of his goods and chattels, together with all his several adventures to the East Indies and Persia, be employed in the purchase of houses in London, the annual profit to be put to charitable use. This included giving 40s. to the churchwardens and collectors for the poor of the parish of Ewell, 'to be distributed among the poor of the said parish'.

Mason's Charity

Mason's Charity dates from 1733 or earlier. Its origins are somewhat obscure, and the records state 'by what instrument given unknown'. In 1894 the investment in Consols was £109 11s. 9d. giving an income of £3. The combined income of Mason's and Dickinson's charities in 1975 was just over £6.

114. The Thomas Brumfield/Helena Fendall memorial was moved from the old church. Their only connection is that they both founded charities.

Thomas Brumfield

Thomas Brumfield made charitable bequests in a will that was proved in 1771 stating that, '£350 to be invested and the income paid to the Vicar for afternoon sermons. Five shares in the Sun Fire Office, £12 of the income to go to the education of 12 poor children of the Parish in reading, writing and accounts, and the remainder to go to clothing six poor widows'.

In 1882 the Charity Commissioners regulated the bequest by a scheme in which the first charge on the income was an annual payment of £12 to the Vicar of St Mary's for afternoon sermons, together with the expenses and salary of a clerk, the balance being divided between relief of the needy and educational assistance. Under the scheme £500 was contributed out of capital for the enlargement of the National School.

David White

The David White Foundation dates from 1751. In 1777 the capital consisted of just under £2,000 in South Sea Stock, the proportion of the income payable to Ewell being £8 8s., 'To teach children belonging to the parish to read and write'. After the National School was established in 1816 the money went to the school. The David White Foundation has been amalgamated with Brumfield's Educational Foundation and the combined income in 1989 was just over £1,000.

Helena Fendall

In her will of 1798, Helena Fendall left £1,000 in trust 'for poor widows and families, or other necessitous persons in the parish of Ewell, not in receipt of poor relief, no case to receive more than £15 annually'. The income in 1975 was just under £60. Helena Fendall lived at Ewell House and died in 1799 at the age of ninety-nine.

Mary de Teissier

By a will of 1848 Mary de Teissier left £90 in Consols, the income to be used to keep in repair her sister's tomb. The balance, if any, was to go to four poor women who had received the Sacrament three times in the year. The income in 1989 was £21.

Thomas Calverley

Thomas Calverley of Ewell Castle stated in his will that he wished the National School House premises to be for the use of the Parish for ever, subject to confirmation by his heir, Hector Monro, his nephew-in-law, a legal necessity in the case of a gift of land by will to charitable uses. Hector Monro was willing to confirm the gift, but he died before it could be implemented, and his son, also Hector Monro, was less public spirited. After considerable argument with the Vestry £200 was given to the Parish to be invested for the benefit of the National School by a trust declared in 1860.

The income in 1989 was just over £40.

115. Between the two World Wars the memorial to those who fell in the 1914-18 conflict was on the Watch House in Church Street. The Ewell Old Boys' Association, with its president Sir Arthur Glyn, seen on the extreme right, paid its respects to its dead comrades.

116. The war memorial in St Mary's churchyard carries the names of the victims of the First World War. A reference to the Second World War has been added, but the names of the fallen are in a Book of Remembrance at the Town Hall.

Thomas Henry Bridges

Thomas Henry Bridges left £1,000 in Consols to the vicar and churchwardens by a will proved in 1862, the income from which they were to distribute 'amongst such poor persons inhabitants of the Parish in such proportion and manner in all respects as the Minister and Churchwardens shall in their discretion think proper'. The income in 1975 was just over £30.

Other Ewell Charities

The Sunday Entertainments Act of 1932 permitted Sunday opening of cinemas, provided some of the profits went to charity. The Epsom and Ewell Borough Council set up the local administration in 1938, the first allocation to Ewell Parochial Charities being made in December, 1941. The Act is no longer in operation and the final distribution was made in 1967. However, there is still income from the fund's investment amounting to over £500 in 1989.

The Ewell War Memorial Maintenance Trust was started by Thomas Martin, a bank manager, who left £200 in Consols by a deed of trust in 1922 to provide for the 'maintenance and upkeep of the Ewell War Memorial which has been erected in the Churchyard of Ewell and of the garden and wall thereof'. The income in 1989 was just under £60.

The Administration of Charities Today

With the advent of the Local Government Act of 1894, the administration of charities, which had been the role of the vicar, churchwardens and overseers of the poor, was taken over by the parish councils. Following the absorption of Ewell into Epsom and Ewell in 1933 trustees were appointed to administer the charities. There has been some rationalisation and amalgamation of the charities and they are now operated under the Ewell Parochial Trusts (Relief in Need). The Board includes three co-opted members with special knowledge of the Ancient Parish of Ewell. Subsidiary trusts are the Ewell Educational Foundation and the Ewell Ecclesiastical Charity.

Chapter 14

Buildings of Ewell

The Appendix lists some of the more outstanding of the many interesting old buildings of Ewell. Here we provide additional information on a few buildings.

Bourne Hall

Although it is no longer there, the Georgian mansion that stood on the site of the present Bourne Hall is worthy of mention. It was built *c*.1770 for Philip Rowden, a well-to-do vintner, who, like many London merchants of the period, wished to have a country house within easy travelling distance of the City. He had acquired the land piecemeal over a period of a few years. Rowden's new house does not appear to have had a name originally and was referred to as the seat of Philip Rowden Esq. Philip Rowden died in 1795, eight years after his wife, and as he seems to have had no direct descendants the property was sold on behalf of his beneficiaries. In his will drafted in 1794 Philip Rowden gave instructions for the disposal of his possessions in great detail, down to his silver teaspoons, tea tongs and silver cream jug. He did not forget the poor and left two chaldrons of coal to those not in the workhouse. Actually, two chaldrons is rather more than one might think and amounts to about two tons. Six poor men and six poor widows were to be given five shillings apiece for attending his memorial service. His coach horses were to be killed immediately after his decease.

117. The gateway and lodge of Bourne Hall, formerly Garbrand Hall, were part of the Hercey Barritt extensions. There is no evidence to support the local tradition that the dog portrays a particular hound that saved a member of the Garbrand family from drowning, nor that the tail is a cow's horn.

Rowden's house was bought in 1796 by Thomas Hercey Barritt, a descendant of a Cornish family who had made good in Jamaica. During the ownership of Barritt considerable changes were made to the mansion: conservatories were added at each end, the gardens were extended and a barn, brewhouse and dairy were built. The dairy which was designed by Henry Kitchen, the architect of Ewell Castle, later became known as The Turrets. An imposing gateway was erected, crowned by a talbot, which forms part of the Barritt coat of arms. There seems to be no evidence to support the local tradition that it portrays a particular hound which saved a member of the family from drowning, nor that the tail is a cow's horn. The arms incorporate those of the Garbrand family with whom the Barritts had intermarried, and the house became known as Garbrand Hall. Thomas Hercey Barritt died in 1817 and after the death of his wife in 1841 the house was sold to Henry Batson, who in 1859 sold it to George Torr, a charcoal manufacturer. George Torr was a great benefactor to Ewell: his gifts included a Willis organ for the church. He died in 1867 at the aged of 52, leaving his widow to carry on running the house. She was a keen gardener and with her head gardener, James Child, won many awards for plants such as azaleas, chrysanthemums and orchids. According to the *Journal of Horticulture and Cottage Gardener* of 14 August 1879, 'Garbrand Hall, Ewell, the residence of Mrs. Torr, is famed for the excellent plants, especially azaleas, which Mr. Child grows so well and exhibits so successfully. But there is much to admire in Mrs. Torr's garden besides the specimen plants. The grounds are about 15 acres in extent and have been made the most of by judicious arrangement. Shrubs, conifers and ornamental trees have been planted in profusion'.

118. A photograph of a coloured engraving of Garbrand Hall, drawn and engraved by J. Hassell and published in March 1817.

119. Garbrand Hall in 1895. It was built around 1770 and acquired by Thomas Hercey Barritt in 1796. Barritt was responsible for extensions which included conservatories at each end.

120. The dairy of Garbrand Hall, later known as The Turrets, was designed in 1810 by Henry Kitchen who was 17 years of age.

121. The late 18th-century Garbrand Hall, later known as Bourne Hall, was demolished and replaced by the community centre and library which opened in 1970. The new Bourne Hall has a large unsupported dome and as well as the library it also houses a museum, lecture hall and facilities for conferences.

122. The lower gallery at the museum houses mainly large industrial bygones.

123. The Bourne Hall Museum opened in 1970. The upper gallery displays a wide range of artefacts, mostly with local connections.

Garbrand Hall remained in the possession of the Torr family until 1896. It then had a variety of owners until 1925 when it was bought by Miss Margaret Glyn, without whose intervention the whole estate might well have been sold off to developers. The name was changed to Bourne Hall and it then became a girls' boarding school, 'for the daughters of gentlemen'. Cases are known of the daughters of high-class tradesmen being refused admission. Through the lease, Miss Glyn insisted on the grounds being kept in good order. Although by this time Bourne Hall had been purchased by the borough council, the proprietor of the school was responsible for repairs and was scared off by the high cost. The girls arrived for the autumn term in 1953 and found the school shut: it did not re-open. There was much discussion and argument about what to do with the building involving the borough council and the county council. It was eventually decided that it had deteriorated so much that restoration and preservation were no longer possible and in 1962 it was demolished and replaced by the present community centre which was opened in 1970. In the words of Mabel Dexter of the Nonsuch Antiquarian Society, 'The outside of the new building is unobtrusive rather than imposing. It rests comfortably on its mound above the lake and is at its best when glimpsed through the greenery of the still beautiful grounds'.

Ewell Castle

Ewell Castle was the largest house in Ewell. It was built for Thomas Calverley in 1810-14 by Henry Kitchen and still stands, although it is now a school. Henry Kitchen was a local boy whose father was a carpenter and the family house was in Church Street. He became a pupil of Jeffrey Wyatt, or Sir Jeffrey Wyattville as he later became, who had designed Nonsuch Mansion, and went on to modify Windsor Castle. At the age of 17 Henry Kitchen designed the dairy for Garbrand Hall. By 1813, at the age of 20, he was practising on his own and had a design for Ewell Castle accepted. In 1816 he emigrated to Australia, where he died at the age of 29, having been unsuccessful in establishing himself over there.

124. A photograph of a coloured print that bears the inscription 'Ewell Castle. The Seat of Thomas Calverley Esq. To whom this print is most respectfully dedicated by his obedient servant, Jas Hardy.'

125. An interior view of Ewell Castle shortly before it became a boys' school in 1926.

126. Ewell Castle was built in 1810-14 by Henry Kitchen for Thomas Calverley, who owned the three sub-manors of Ewell. It was the biggest house in Ewell, described in 1917 as a noble castellated mansion with 45 acres of ground. The by-pass constructed in the 1930s cut through the grounds.

127. The Ewell Castle sales catalogue of 1917 referred to the Japanese water garden as the most beautiful in England.

Having inherited the three sub-manors of Ewell, and acquiring even more property by the Enclosure Act of 1801, Thomas Calverley was the biggest land owner in Ewell, so it was fitting that he should have a grand house. He died in 1842 and was succeeded by his nephew, Hector William Bower Monro, but he died in the month following coming into his inheritance and the estate passed to his son. In 1852 it was conveyed to James Gadesden from Yorkshire whose family held Ewell Castle until 1902. There are numerous memorials and tombs for the Calverleys and Gadesdens in and around St Mary's Church. In 1917 Ewell Castle was sold by auction for the then owner, Captain C. Wiener. Clarence Wiener was an American of Austrian origin and as the First World War was in progress was regarded with so much suspicion that he sued Associated Newspapers for libel in respect of articles that they had published concerning Ewell Castle. They had alleged, among other things, that in the gardens were deep concrete foundations which could be used in case of invasion as emplacements for enemy guns directed against London. Wiener maintained that the concrete formed the bed of an artificial lake. In spite of having the eminent Mr. Marshall Hall K.C. as his counsel, the damages awarded to Wiener amounted to only £50 against the *Evening News* and £25 against *The People*. In the sales catalogue the buildings, contents and grounds are described in 18 pages of purple prose which referred to a noble castellated mansion with 45 acres of ground. There was an Adam-style dining room, a grand staircase, an indoor palm court, billiard room, library and museum; the grounds contained tennis courts, a bowling green, a full-sized polo ground and a golf course; the Japanese water garden was the most beautiful in England. Since 1926 Ewell Castle has been a boys' school.

Watch House

The Watch House in Church Street was built towards the end of the 18th century and served the dual purpose of fire engine house and lock-up. The fire engine, referred to as being old in 1770, was last used at a fire at 15 High Street in about 1867. Unless it was sufficiently near the river or pond to use its suction hose, its tanks had to be filled by buckets of water. With a team of men operating the pump it could throw water as high as any house in the village. The fire engine has been retired to Bourne Hall Museum. The Watch House carried the war memorial between the world wars and was the venue for the remembrance service. The memorial was re-erected by the spring head known as the Dipping Place at the entrance to Bourne Hall.

128. The fire engine, which in 1770 was described as old, was kept in one half of the Watch House. This shows it towards the end of the last century.

129. The fire engine is now in the Bourne Hall Museum. With a team of men working the pump it could throw a powerful jet of water.

130. Ewell Fire Brigade in 1907 with a bigger engine which was kept in the building shown, now (1992) the Launderette in the High Street.

131. Spring House in Spring Street dates from about 1740 and is clad in mathematical tiles (brick tiles). It is unusual in that the tiles were put on when it was first built; they were frequently added to existing houses.

132. The *Spring Hotel*, seen here early this century, is thought to have been a farmhouse which became an inn when coaches began to pass as a result of alterations of the roads in 1834 so that London to Epsom traffic no longer had to use the narrow Church Street.

133. The present day *Spring Hotel* is still popular.

134. Several old houses in Ewell are faced with mathematical tiles. This display in Bourne Hall Museum shows how they were used. It was donated to the museum in 1981 when a symposium on mathematical tiles chaired by Alec Clifton Taylor was held in Ewell.

Spring House

Ewell has several houses with walls of mathematical tiles.¹ Spring House, in Spring Street, dates from about 1740 and has a central bay window and a doorway with Tuscan columns and pediment. The shape of the bay relates to the octagonal rooms inside, which created something of a problem when it was wished to divide the rooms into smaller ones.

The *Spring Hotel*

The *Spring Hotel* is thought to be an early 19th-century farmhouse that became an inn when the road was built in 1834 to take the London to Epsom traffic away from Church Street. Mention of the inn leads to a reference to Derby Week, which used to be the great event of the year in Ewell. Cloudesley Willis gave a lively account of how it was towards the end of the last century in which he described the varied stream of vehicles and people that jammed the village on the way to the races, a social mix from costermongers to princes. The takings at the *Spring Hotel* during a good Derby week would pay the rent for the year. 'King Edward VII, when Prince of Wales, has been held up in Ewell High Street for a quarter of an hour or more ...The windows were full of people watching the procession and the fun'. Modern-day Ewell does not welcome the Derby Day crowds with quite so much enthusiasm: it locks its doors.

135. Before the bypass was built Derby Day always brought plenty of traffic through Ewell. This shows it in 1931.

Chapter 15

Ewell in the 20th century

To bring this history up to date, some reference must be made to events in the 20th century. Until the end of the First World War the Ewell of 1881 pictured in Chapter 10 would not have changed a great deal. The social pattern was still largely that of a rural community: a small number of gentry with their servants, a few farmers and millers and a mass of poorer families providing labour. After 1918 things changed rapidly as the motor car took over the roads and the rail services increased with electrification. Today, Ewell is essentially a dormitory suburb and a part of Epsom, with a corresponding social pattern.

The years since 1918 have seen great changes in the appearance of the town: many old buildings have been rebuilt and there has been much infilling. Large houses in their own grounds have been replaced by a multitude of small dwellings and blocks of flats, the Old Fair Field has disappeared under bricks and mortar, the 18th-century Bourne Hall has been replaced by a giant upturned saucer in concrete. The heart of the 'village' suffered particularly from the destruction of interesting old buildings in the 1960s. The late 17th-century Ewell House was demolished in 1960. 1962 saw the destruction of Bourne Hall and Carpenter's Bakery in the High Street, a late medieval building that had been a baker's since 1817. The Bourne Hall dairy and brewhouse, known as The Turrets, came down in 1967 and the 16th-century timber-framed Nuttall's grocers shop in Cheam Road disappeared in 1968. The changes in Ewell have not all been environmentally negative: the local council have been able to turn private land into public parks, two outstanding examples being the grounds of Bourne Hall and Ewell Court.

136. The *Lord Nelson*, seen here in 1905, was built at the turn of the century on the site of an earlier public house in the High Street. It was demolished in 1963 and replaced by Barclays Bank and a row of shops.

137. The Elms, later renamed The Grange, was in London Road where St Mary's Close now is. William Thomas Carlisle was the owner at the time of his death in 1892. This picture was taken soon after that date.

Like most other towns and villages, Ewell lost many of its men in the 1914-1918 war; the memorial by the Dipping Place lists 80 names. In the Second World War civilians as well as the armed forces were in the front line. The war memorial in the churchyard refers to the two world wars but the names listed are only for the First World War. The Book of Remembrance kept at the Town Hall records the dead of the later war. The number of service people from Epsom and Ewell killed in the Second World War was nearly three hundred. In addition, 43 people were killed in air raids in Epsom and Ewell and hundreds were injured. Nearly 200 houses were destroyed and 12,000 damaged. In the three month period from 9 September to 11 December 1940, 380 high explosive and 1,265 incendiary bombs fell on the borough. There was major damage in Ewell in June 1944 when houses were demolished by a flying bomb at the Kingston Road end of Timbercroft.

One of the things that has changed considerably in recent years is the flow of the Hogsmill, which was a sizeable river when Millais featured it in his painting, *Ophelia in the Stream*. However, because of reduced rainfall and increased pumping of water from boreholes in the chalk, the flow is no longer 4½ million gallons a day, in fact it has almost ceased and the Hogsmill is no longer noted for its trout. Today, Ophelia would suffer nothing worse than a mud bath.

Whereas the flow of water in the Hogsmill has diminished, the flow of vehicles along the roads has grown to flood level. The building of the bypass in the mid-1930s relieved the centre of Ewell of much of the through traffic, until overloading of the new road led to attempts to avoid the bypass by going through the village. It is to be hoped that the widening of the bypass, recently completed, will bring about some improvement.

Chapter 16

The Enigmas of Ewell

Mrs. Jordan

I should not like to close this account of Ewell without reference to three rather intriguing enigmas that have been encountered. Tradition has it that Mrs. Jordan, the actress and the mistress of William IV when he was the Duke of Clarence, lived in Church Street in a house on the site of the Red House. The Duke would visit her there and was fond of calling on Mr. Charles Hall of the Upper Mill and looking at his white cattle. Mrs. Jordan was apparently a woman of considerable character. On one occasion, when the Duke wrote proposing to reduce her allowance, she replied by sending him the torn-off bottom of a playbill, which said, 'No money returned after the rising of the curtain'. Mrs. Jordan bore the Duke ten children so the curtain must have been raised fairly frequently. I have been unable to find any hard evidence confirming that Mrs. Jordan lived in Church Street.

138. The Red House, Church Street, was built in Queen-Anne style at the beginning of the 20th century.

The Tunnels of Ewell

The second enigma is of a rather different type and concerns the tunnels of Ewell. In the vicinity of the site of Ewell House, which was pulled down in 1960, is an elaborate system of tunnels, with several entrances, now blocked off. When the tunnels were explored by members of the Chelsea Speliological Society in 1962 they reported that they were four to six feet wide and mostly on the same level, with a roof thickness of between six and twelve feet, approximately half of the total length having been carefully brick lined. The longest branch explored in 1962 was about 250 feet but they could well have been longer originally.

There are two major questions: when were the tunnels built and why? Ewell House was built

139. The rear of Ewell House, West Street, in 1958. Parts of the house dated back to the late 17th century. It was demolished in 1960. In the grounds were some enigmatic tunnels.

in the late 17th century and some believe that the tunnels were excavated at that time. Others believe that they are as recent as 1870.

The theories as to the purpose of the tunnels are varied and include a distribution point for smugglers, a secret link to Ewell Castle and a folly made by an owner of Ewell House just for fun.

The tunnels served a useful purpose in the Second World War: they were used as an air raid shelter. Their origin and intended use are a subject for conjecture.

Bluebird

Soon after we arrived in Ewell in 1982 we were taken around the village by one of our new friends who pointed out a short length of railway track under an arched gatehouse in West Street and said that Sir Malcolm Campbell's Bluebird had been built there. Other people in the village were sure there was a connection with Bluebird, but were unable to offer evidence. On enquiry we found that the area had been the site of the factory of J. L. Jameson Ltd., an engineering company that started in Ewell in 1933 and was there until the early 1960s when they moved to Chessington to a factory they had opened there in about 1950. Jameson's made a wide range of specialised heavy duty machine tools, and prototypes of such things as the under-carriage of the Valiant bomber. They also made an aero engine — the Jameson Flat Four. During the Second World War as many as 180 people worked in the West Street premises. Our informant had worked for the company during most of its period in Ewell: he had no knowledge of any connection with Bluebird. If there was a Bluebird connection one would expect it to be with Jameson's and so the matter remains an enigma.

Last Words

Anyone looking at a photograph of Ewell as it was 50 years ago must regret the disappearance of so many attractive old buildings: fortunately, the centre of the village is now under a conservation order. Although much has been lost, sufficient remains to point to the long and interesting history and provide a focus for continuing documentary and archaeological research. With regard to Roman Ewell there is much still to be done. The Roman Villa Group of the Surrey Archaeological Society, which has a number of members living in Ewell, is compiling a Gazetteer of the excavations that have been carried out in the area; this will enable plans to be made for further study and digs to add to the existing body of knowledge. The aim is to establish the boundaries of the Romano-British settlement, and whether it was one of the Stane Street posting stations.There is an active Antiquarian Society and an excellent local museum: Old Ewell lives on.

Notes

Chapter One: The Development of the Parish
1. The use of the past tense is necessary in view of the present state of the Hogsmill River as referred to in Chapter 15.

Chapter Four: Saxon Ewell
1. Various alternative spellings are known including, 'Euuelle' (Saxon), 'Ewelle' (1155), Yewell (1603). The Domesday spelling 'Etwelle' is considered to have been a mistake made by the scribe, since the 't' does not occur elsewhere.

Chapter Five: Medieval Ewell and the Manors
1. Merton was an Augustinian priory founded by Gilbert the Knight after a grant of land by Henry I in 1114. It received many subsequent gifts and in 1242 it held more than 200 estates in 16 different counties.
2. Chertsey was a Benedictine Abbey founded by Erkenwald in 675, sacked by Viking raiders in 871 and re-colonised in 964.
3. Newark was an Augustinian priory founded in the late 12th century.
4. Southwark, Ewell and Guildford were in the diocese of Winchester; Croydon was in the diocese of Canterbury.
5. The Saunder family was important in Surrey and already held several estates when the Ewell property was acquired. There was a strong Catholic tradition among the numerous branches, and various members were listed as recusants.

Chapter Six: Tudor Ewell and the Palace of Nonsuch
1. In 1960 some of the local volunteers formed the Nonsuch and Ewell Antiquarian Society, which in 1973 became the Nonsuch Antiquarian Society.

Chapter Seven: The Mid-17th Century
1. The John Dent account is supported by the wording of the *Memoirs of the Two Last Years of the Reign of King Charles I*, by Sir Thomas Herbert, Groom of the Chambers to his Majesty. '... they were engaged by Colonel Rich his Regiment of Horse, and after a sharp Skirmish, forc'd to retreat back towards Kingston, and to make good a Pass between Ewell and Nonsuch-Park, the Fight was on either side maintained with extraordinary Fierceness and Valour, in which there were many Gentlemen slain on both sides, amongst which was the Lord Francis Villiers, who that day expressed much Courage, and as the report goes, was offer'd but refused Quarter'. At the time of this encounter the King was confined in Carisbrooke Castle by the Roundheads, Thomas Herbert being with him, so his account carries less weight than some of the other contemporary reports.

Chapter Eight: Administration and the Poor
1. Acts making the destruction of troublesome birds a statutory duty can be traced back at least to 1532.

Chapter Nine: The Glyn Family and the Church
1. John Taylor was born in Gloucester in 1580. He was apprenticed to a London waterman, but was seized by the press gang and spent several years at sea before returning to the Thames as a waterman. He went on to become a writer of pamphlets on current events and a poet. His comments on the state of the clergy in Ewell are given in his pamphlet 'The Unnatural Father', an account of a sad murder in Ewell in 1621 when one John Rowse drowned his two children in 'an excellent spring of water in the cellar of his house', since he could offer them nothing but a life of poverty. The unnatural father was hanged at Croydon 'where he dyed with great penitency and remorce of Conscience'. John Taylor died in 1653, having written his own epitaph in typical poetic style:

> Here lies the Water Poet, Honest John,
> Who rowed in streams of Helicon,
> Where having rocks and dangers passed,
> He at the haven of Heaven arrived at last.

2. Richard Glyn was Lord Mayor of London in 1758 and became a baronet in 1759. He was one of the founder members of Glyn Mills Bank.
3. Sir George Glyn lived in considerable style, as evidenced by the specification of a new carriage he ordered in 1808, which was to be 'a new neat Landau on a Perch carriage with a sail forward platform to the fore part ... Painted Princess Yellow with handsome mantles and arms on all the panels. Crests on the rails and mouldings picked out in black, the carriage and wheels the same colour and varnished, the upper part covered with best neats leather with plated beads, silver embossed crest head plates ... best plate glasses ... Trunks under the seats and a carpet to the bottom completed with best materials and work-manship'. The price taking into account an allowance of £25 'for the old chariot' was £286 14s.0d. That was a large sum of money in 1808: the modern equivalent of this carriage would be at least a Rolls.
4. Henry Clutton of Hartswood (1814-1895), not to be confused with Henry Clutton (1819-1893), who went into partnership with the architect Burgess and was selected as architect for the Roman Catholic Cathedral of Westminster. It was not however built to his design as he died before work started and it was finally built by J. F. Bentley.
5. Both Holman Hunt and his friend John Millais had connections with Ewell. An uncle of the former, William Hobman, lived at Rectory Farm, while Millais was friendly with the Lempriere family of Worcester Park Farm. Ewell was sufficiently rural in those days to provide the painters with material for their countryside scenes. Millais used the Hogsmill River with its abundance of wild flowers as the 'glassy stream' in which Ophelia had 'too much of water', in his *Ophelia in the Stream*.

Chapter Ten: Ewell in 1881
1. The Sheep Fair was of particular importance and large numbers of sheep would be driven down from the Downs. The fairs were held in a meadow behind the *Green Man*, called the Fair Field. The *Green Man* gets its first mention in the parish vestry accounts for 1763; it was one of the public houses to which members of the vestry retired at the end of the meetings. The present building dates from the 1930s.
2. A licence to hold a market in Ewell was granted to Henry Lloyd, lord of the manor, in 1618. It was held on Thursdays, but seems to have been discontinued early in the 19th century. Although in the absence of a market the Ewell of 1881 could not strictly be described as a market town, its many shops and small businesses must have given it the atmosphere of one.

Chapter Eleven: Industry and Transport
1. Available reports refer to a total of 17 deaths from explosions from 1757 to 1871.*The Gentleman's Magazine* gives the number killed in an explosion in 1768 as five, the highest figure for one explosion. In 1777 a workman was killed by falling into a heap of gunpowder and suffocating.
2. The setting up of turnpike trusts was at its peak in the 1750s, a period that has been referred to as The Turnpike Mania. By the mid-1830s there were more than 20,000 miles of turnpike roads throughout the country. Surrey had about 300 miles. They declined after that date as railways were built.
3. The Railways Act of 1921, laid down that the railways of Great Britain were to be merged into four groups. The Southern Group included the L.S.W. Railway and the L.B.S.C. Railway. The L.B.S.C.R. started electrification in 1905 using a high voltage overhead wire system. The L.S.W.R. started using a third rail system in 1915, and this was the system adopted for the whole of the Southern Group after 1921. The overhead wire system is the one commonly used nowadays for main-line services in other areas.

Chapter Fourteen: Buildings of Ewell
1. One of the several alternative names for the mathematical tile is brick tile, which is quite appropriate for a tile made to look like a brick. The tiles are so shaped that when hung together on a wall and pointed they look like a brick wall.They were most commonly used in the south east in the 18th and 19th centuries, usually as an addition to an existing timber-framed building to improve weather resistance and ape the fashionable brick. Contrary to what is sometimes believed, mathematical tiles were not introduced as an attempt to escape the brick tax. The tax covered tiles as well as bricks and only marginal savings would have been possible. Spring House is unusual in that the tiles were employed in the original construction.

Appendix

The Old Buildings of Ewell

Ewell has a considerable number of Grade II Listed Buildings, i.e. buildings of such historic interest that they should not be demolished without very good reason. The following are some of the more outstanding:

Cheam Road
Pit House. Large house, 18th century extended in 19th, now part of garden centre.

Chessington Road
Ewell West Railway Station. The original two-storey station. The railway opened in 1859.
Fitznell's Manor House. Early 17th century, three-gabled addition to remnant of early 16th-century manor house. Converted to offices in 1989.

Church Street
Watch House. Single-storey building of the late 18th century with later modifications.
Well House. Early 18th century, three storey, red brick.
Ewell Castle. Two-storey battlemented mansion by Henry Kitchen in 1810-1814, now a boys' school.
Rectory Farm Barn. 18th-century weather-boarded barn that stands behind Barn House.
Glyn House. Large brick house by Henry Duesbury, 1839.
Old Church Tower. Early 15th-century remnant of the old church that was demolished when the present St. Mary's church was built. (The tower is an Ancient Monument.)
Church Street has several 18th-century houses faced with mathematical tiles.

Ewell Bypass
Banqueting House plinth. Brick retaining walls of plinth on which the banqueting house of Nonsuch Palace stood. Some 16th-century brickwork, remainder restored at various periods.

Ewell Court Avenue
Packhorse Bridge. Narrow brick bridge without a parapet that crosses a branch of the Hogsmill River.18th century restored at various periods.

High Street
No. 9. Early 16th-century timber framed building, once an inn.
Nos. 11-15 (including north corner of Church Street). Timber framed buildings with a jettied part dating from *c*.1550 and the remainder around 1600.
No. 17 (south corner of Church Street). 17th-century building.
King William IV public house. Early 19th century.
No. 26 (corner of High Street and West Street). 17th-century building with mathematical tiles

added in the 18th century.
No. 31 (corner of Cheam Road and the High Street). Twin-gabled building, late 16th century.
There are numerous 18th-century buildings in the High Street.

Kingston Road
Lower Mill House. 17-18th centuries.
Nos. 25 and 27. 18th-century weather-boarded cottages.

London Road
Spring Hotel. Early 19th century, brick/weather-boarded.
St. Mary's church. 1847-8 by Henry Clutton. Gothic Revival.

Mill Lane
Numbers 3 to 13. Late 18th - early 19th century weather-boarded cottages.

Spring Street
Bourne Hall Dog Gate. Entrance gateway topped by heraldic talbot. Early 19th century.
Bourne Hall Lodge. Small early 19th-century lodge house.
Bourne Hall Bridge. Bridge with semi-circular arch at end of lake. Late 18th century.
Chessington Lodge. Two-storey, 18th-century house clad with mathematical tiles.
Spring House. Three-storey mid 18th-century house clad with mathematical tiles.
Chessington House. Two-storey early 18th-century house, clad with mathematical tiles.

West Street
1861 School. Two-storey red brick with gables, no longer used as a school.
Harwood House (No. 63). Two storeys plus attics. Late 17th century.

Bibliography

Albert, William, *The Turnpike Road System in England 1663-1840*, (C.U.P., 1972).

Allen, Thomas, *History of the Counties of Surrey and Sussex*, (1829).

Audeley, Major Lewis, *A True Relation of the Great Victory of the Parliaments Forces against those of Surrey*, (1648).

Bates, Alan, *Directory of Stage Coach Services 1836*, (David and Charles, 1969).

Chelsea Speleological Society Records, vol. 3, 1963.

Deedes, C., ed., *Register or Memorial of Ewell*, (Mitchell, Hughes & Clarke, 1913).

Dent, John, *The Quest for Nonsuch*, (Hutchinson & Co. Ltd., 1970).

English Place Name Society, *The Place Names of Surrey*, vol. XI (C.U.P., 1934).

Exwood, M., and West I. J., *Mathematical Tiles in Surrey, Surrey History*, vol. II no. 5, (Phillimore for the Surrey Local History Council, 1983/84).

Farries, K. G., and Mason, M. T., *The Windmills of Surrey and Inner London*, (Charles Skilton Ltd., 1966).

Harrison, J. F. C., *The Common People*, (Fontana, 1984).

Herbert, Sir Thomas, *Memoirs of the two last years of the reign of King Charles I*, written in 1678, published by G. and W. Nicol, 1813).

Lowther, A. W. G., *Excavations at Purberry Shot, Ewell, Surrey, Surrey Archaeological Collections*, vol. 50 (The Surrey Archaeological Society, 1946).

Malden, H. E., ed., *The Victoria History of the County of Surrey*, (Archibald Constable and Co., 1902).

Manning, O. and Bray, W., *The History and Antiquities of the County of Surrey*, (1804-14).

Margary, Ivan D., *Roman Ways in the Weald*, (Phoenix House, 1965).

Marshall, C. F. Dendy, *History of the Southern Railway*, (Ian Allen Ltd., 1968).

Meekings, C. A. F., and Shearman, P., ed., *Fitznell's Cartulary*, (Surrey Record Society, 1968).

Nonsuch Antiquarian Society Publications, occasional papers.
   No. 5 Buildings in Ewell.
   No. 6 Bells of St. Mary's, Ewell.
   No.12 Ewell Pauper Examinations and Bastardy Papers, 1617 - 1809.
   No.13 The Letters of Anna Glyn, 1892.
   No.14 Caring for the Ewell Poor before 1838.
   No.15 Ewell Public Houses in History.
   No.16 19th Century Boys at School.

Rose, Michael E., *The English Poor Law 1780-1930*, (David and Charles, 1971).

Shearman, P., *Ewell in 1577, Surrey Archaeological Collections*, vol. 54 (The Surrey Archaeological Society, 1955).

Stenton, Sir Frank, *Anglo Saxon England, The Oxford History of England*, (O.U.P., 3rd edn.,1989).

Trueblood, Walter, *The Story of Ewell Congregational Church, 1865-1965*, (Raynes Park Press, 1965).

Turner, J. T. Howard, *The London, Brighton and South Coast Railway*, (Batsford, 1978).

Walker, M. L., *The Manor of Batailles and the Family of Saunder in Ewell during the 16th and 17th Centuries, Surrey Archaeological Collections*, vol. 54 (The Surrey Archaeological Society, 1955).

Willis, Cloudesley, S., *A Short History of Ewell and Nonsuch*, (Pullingers Ltd., 1931, revised 1948).

Winbolt, S. E., *With a Spade on Stane Street*, (Methuen, 1936).

Index

Figures in bold refer to illustrations